Cooking Soups For Dummies®

W9-BZX-512

Cheat Sheet

Basic Equipment

You need the following items to begin building the foundation of your soup-cooking arena:

- 4½- to 6-quart heavy Dutch oven with lid
- 1½-quart saucepan with lid
- 2½- to 3-quart saucepan with lid
- 10-inch skillet (the Dutch oven's lid may fit)
- 8- to 10-quart stock pot with lid (optional)
- 3- to 4-inch paring knife
- 6- to 8-inch chef's knife for chopping
- Serrated knife for slicing bread and tomatoes
- 8- to 10-inch slicing knife (optional)
- Carving or large kitchen fork
- Sharpening steel
- Sharpening stone or knife sharpener
- Baking sheet
- Can and bottle opener
- Colander
- Cooling rack

- Cutting boards
- Grater, preferably four-sided
- Measuring cup set, for both dry and liquid ingredients
- Measuring spoons
- Mixing bowls
- Sieves (medium diameter, one fine mesh and one medium mesh)
- Storage containers for freezer and refrigerator with covers and/or self-sealing plastic storage bags
- Ladle
- Skimmer
- Spoons (wooden, slotted, and solid)
- Tongs
- Vegetable peeler
- Wine opener

Freezing Times for Soups and Broths

Type of Soup	Freezing Time
Broth	Up to 6 months
Pureed vegetable soups	Up to 3 months
Legume soups	Up to 2 months
Creamy soups	Up to 2 months
Brothy, multi-ingredient soups	1 to 2 months
Seafood soups	Best eaten fresh or within 3 days

Cooking Soups For Dummies®

Seasoning

You'll need these flavorful ingredients for the soup recipes in this book:

Spices

- Allspice (whole berries and ground)
- Caraway seeds
- Cardamom (whole and ground)
- Cayenne or ground red chili pepper
- Cloves (whole and ground)
- Chili powder
- Crushed red chili flakes
- Cinnamon (sticks and ground)
- Coriander (ground or whole)
- Cumin (ground)
- Curry powder, preferably Madras style
- Mustard, dried English style
- Nutmeg (preferably whole so it can be freshly grated; otherwise, ground)
- Paprika and/or Hungarian sweet paprika
- Black peppercorns (to be freshly ground)
- White pepper (ground or white peppercorns)
- Turmeric

Herbs

- Basil
- Bay leaf
- Chives
- Cilantro, fresh
- Dill, fresh
- Mint, fresh
- Oregano
- Parsley, fresh (preferably flat-leaf)
- Rosemary
- Thyme leaves

Others flavorings

- Dijon mustard
- Chinese sesame oil
- Chinese chili oil
- Salt (kosher, fine-grained, or sea salt)
- Sherry
- Soy sauce
- Tabasco or other liquid hot red pepper sauce
- Thai fish sauce
- Vermouth, dry white
- Wine vinegar, rice wine, and/or white wine
- Worcestershire sauce

Copyright © 2001 IDG Books Worldwide, Inc. All rights reserved.

Cheat Sheet $2.95 value. Item 6333-5.

For more information about IDG Books, call 1-800-762-2974.

For Dummies™: Bestselling Book Series for Beginners

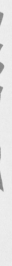

Cooking Soups FOR DUMMIES®

by Jenna Holst

Photographs by David Bishop

IDG Books Worldwide, Inc.
An International Data Group Company

Foster City, CA ◆ Chicago, IL ◆ Indianapolis, IN ◆ New York, NY

Cooking Soups For Dummies®

Published by
IDG Books Worldwide, Inc.
An International Data Group Company
919 E. Hillsdale Blvd.
Suite 300
Foster City, CA 94404
www.idgbooks.com (IDG Books Worldwide Web site)
www.dummies.com (Dummies Press Web site)

Library of Congress Control Number: 00-11196

ISBN: 0-7645-6333-5

Printed in the United States of America

10 9 8 7 6 5 4 3 2 1

1B/RR/QR/QR/IN

Distributed in the United States by IDG Books Worldwide, Inc.

Distributed by CDG Books Canada Inc. for Canada; by Transworld Publishers Limited in the United Kingdom; by IDG Norge Books for Norway; by IDG Sweden Books for Sweden; by IDG Books Australia Publishing Corporation Pty. Ltd. for Australia and New Zealand; by TransQuest Publishers Pte Ltd. for Singapore, Malaysia, Thailand, Indonesia, and Hong Kong; by Gotop Information Inc. for Taiwan; by ICG Muse, Inc. for Japan; by Intersoft for South Africa; by Eyrolles for France; by International Thomson Publishing for Germany, Austria and Switzerland; by Distribuidora Cuspide for Argentina; by LR International for Brazil; by Galileo Libros for Chile; by Ediciones ZETA S.C.R. Ltda. for Peru; by WS Computer Publishing Corporation, Inc., for the Philippines; by Contemporanea de Ediciones for Venezuela; by Express Computer Distributors for the Caribbean and West Indies; by Micronesia Media Distributor, Inc. for Micronesia; by Chips Computadoras S.A. de C.V. for Mexico; by Editorial Norma de Panama S.A. for Panama; by American Bookshops for Finland.

For general information on IDG Books Worldwide's books in the U.S., please call our Consumer Customer Service department at 800-762-2974. For reseller information, including discounts and premium sales, please call our Reseller Customer Service department at 800-434-3422.

For information on where to purchase IDG Books Worldwide's books outside the U.S., please contact our International Sales department at 317-572-3993 or fax 317-572-4002.

For consumer information on foreign language translations, please contact our Customer Service department at 1-800-434-3422, fax 317-572-4002, or e-mail rights@idgbooks.com.

For information on licensing foreign or domestic rights, please phone +1-650-653-7098.

For sales inquiries and special prices for bulk quantities, please contact our Order Services department at 800-434-4322 or write to the address above.

For information on using IDG Books Worldwide's books in the classroom or for ordering examination copies, please contact our Educational Sales department at 800-434-2086 or fax 317-572-4005.

For press review copies, author interviews, or other publicity information, please contact our Public Relations department at 650-653-7000 or fax 650-653-7500.

For authorization to photocopy items for corporate, personal, or educational use, please contact Copyright Clearance Center, 222 Rosewood Drive, Danvers, MA 01923, or fax 978-750-4470.

is a registered trademark under exclusive license to IDG Books Worldwide, Inc., from International Data Group, Inc.

About the Author

Jenna Holst is the author of *Stews* (Macmillan, 1998). Her work has been featured in many national magazines including *Food & Wine, Family Circle, Weight Watchers,* and *Redbook*. She has worked for many years as a food writer, culinary instructor, and consultant. Her clients have included several book publishers as well as PBS and cable television programs. Formerly a resident of New Jersey, she currently lives in South Africa.

ABOUT IDG BOOKS WORLDWIDE

Welcome to the world of IDG Books Worldwide.

IDG Books Worldwide, Inc., is a subsidiary of International Data Group, the world's largest publisher of computer-related information and the leading global provider of information services on information technology. IDG was founded more than 30 years ago by Patrick J. McGovern and now employs more than 9,000 people worldwide. IDG publishes more than 290 computer publications in over 75 countries. More than 90 million people read one or more IDG publications each month.

Launched in 1990, IDG Books Worldwide is today the #1 publisher of best-selling computer books in the United States. We are proud to have received eight awards from the Computer Press Association in recognition of editorial excellence and three from Computer Currents' First Annual Readers' Choice Awards. Our best-selling ...For Dummies® series has more than 50 million copies in print with translations in 31 languages. IDG Books Worldwide, through a joint venture with IDG's Hi-Tech Beijing, became the first U.S. publisher to publish a computer book in the People's Republic of China. In record time, IDG Books Worldwide has become the first choice for millions of readers around the world who want to learn how to better manage their businesses.

Our mission is simple: Every one of our books is designed to bring extra value and skill-building instructions to the reader. Our books are written by experts who understand and care about our readers. The knowledge base of our editorial staff comes from years of experience in publishing, education, and journalism — experience we use to produce books to carry us into the new millennium. In short, we care about books, so we attract the best people. We devote special attention to details such as audience, interior design, use of icons, and illustrations. And because we use an efficient process of authoring, editing, and desktop publishing our books electronically, we can spend more time ensuring superior content and less time on the technicalities of making books.

You can count on our commitment to deliver high-quality books at competitive prices on topics you want to read about. At IDG Books Worldwide, we continue in the IDG tradition of delivering quality for more than 30 years. You'll find no better book on a subject than one from IDG Books Worldwide.

John Kilcullen
Chairman and CEO
IDG Books Worldwide, Inc.

Eighth Annual Computer Press Awards ➤1992

Ninth Annual Computer Press Awards ➤1993

Tenth Annual Computer Press Awards ➤1994

Eleventh Annual Computer Press Awards ➤1995

IDG is the world's leading IT media, research and exposition company. Founded in 1964, IDG had 1997 revenues of $2.05 billion and has more than 9,000 employees worldwide. IDG offers the widest range of media options that reach IT buyers in 75 countries representing 95% of worldwide IT spending. IDG's diverse product and services portfolio spans six key areas including print publishing, online publishing, expositions and conferences, market research, education and training, and global marketing services. More than 90 million people read one or more of IDG's 290 magazines and newspapers, including IDG's leading global brands — Computerworld, PC World, Network World, Macworld and the Channel World family of publications. IDG Books Worldwide is one of the fastest-growing computer book publishers in the world, with more than 700 titles in 36 languages. The "...For Dummies®" series alone has more than 50 million copies in print. IDG offers online users the largest network of technology-specific Web sites around the world through IDG.net (http://www.idg.net), which comprises more than 225 targeted Web sites in 55 countries worldwide. International Data Corporation (IDC) is the world's largest provider of information technology data, analysis and consulting, with research centers in over 41 countries and more than 400 research analysts worldwide. IDG World Expo is a leading producer of more than 168 globally branded conferences and expositions in 35 countries including E3 (Electronic Entertainment Expo), Macworld Expo, ComNet, Windows World Expo, ICE (Internet Commerce Expo), Agenda, DEMO, and Spotlight. IDG's training subsidiary, ExecuTrain, is the world's largest computer training company, with more than 230 locations worldwide and 785 training courses. IDG Marketing Services helps industry-leading IT companies build international brand recognition by developing global integrated marketing programs via IDG's print, online and exposition products worldwide. Further information about the company can be found at www.idg.com.   1/26/00

Dedication

For my mother.

Author's Acknowledgments

Thanks to Pieto, Ansa, Katie, Bruce, Julia della Croce, Linda Ingroia, Tim Gallan, Miriam Goderich, and Jane Dystel.

Publisher's Acknowledgments

We're proud of this book; please register your comments through our IDG Books Worldwide Online Registration Form located at www.dummies.com.

Some of the people who helped bring this book to market include the following:

Acquisitions, Editorial, and Media Development

Senior Project Editor: Tim Gallan

Senior Acquisitions Editor: Linda Ingroia

Copy Editor: Gwenette Gaddis

Technical Reviewer, Recipe Tester: Emily Nolan

Nutrition Analyst: Patty Santelli

Editorial Manager: Pam Mourouzis

Editorial Assistant: Carol Strickland

Production

Project Coordinator: Leslie Alvarez

Layout and Graphics: Amy Adrian, Jacque Schneider, Jeremey Unger, Erin Zeltner

Illustrator: Liz Kurtzman

Photography Design Director: Michele Laseau

Photographer: David Bishop

Food Stylist: Brett Kurzweil

Prop Stylist: Randi Barritt

Proofreaders: Andy Hollandbeck, Nancy Price, Dwight Ramsey, York Production Services, Inc.

Indexer: York Production Services, Inc.

General and Administrative

IDG Books Worldwide, Inc.: John Kilcullen, CEO; Bill Barry, President and COO

IDG Books Consumer Reference Group

Business: Kathleen A. Welton, Vice President and Publisher; Kevin Thornton, Acquisitions Manager

Cooking/Gardening: Jennifer Feldman, Associate Vice President and Publisher

Education/Reference: Diane Graves Steele, Vice President and Publisher; Greg Tubach, Publishing Director

Lifestyles: Kathleen Nebenhaus, Vice President and Publisher; Tracy Boggier, Managing Editor

Pets: Dominique De Vito, Associate Vice President and Publisher; Tracy Boggier, Managing Editor

Travel: Michael Spring, Vice President and Publisher; Suzanne Jannetta, Editorial Director; Brice Gosnell, Managing Editor

IDG Books Consumer Editorial Services: Kathleen Nebenhaus, Vice President and Publisher; Kristin A. Cocks, Editorial Director; Cindy Kitchel, Editorial Director

IDG Books Consumer Production: Debbie Stailey, Production Director

IDG Books Packaging: Marc J. Mikulich, Vice President, Brand Strategy and Research

◆

The publisher would like to give special thanks to Patrick J. McGovern, without whom this book would not have been possible.

◆

Cover photo recipes, from left: New England Clam Chowder, Country Chicken Noodle Soup, Spanish Gazpacho

Contents at a Glance

Cartoons at a Glance

By Rich Tennant

"OK Cookie-your venison in lingonberry sauce is good, as are your eggplant soufflé and the risotto with foie gras. But whoever taught you how to make a croquembouche should be shot!"

page 61

"Oh, I have a very healthy relationship with food. It's the relationship I have with my scale that's not so good."

page 205

"Oooo, what's in here? Is that sun-dried eye of newt? Is that sun-dried eye of newt? How gourmet!"

page 21

Bill and Irwin make vichyssoise

OK- take a leek...

Let me drink some water first.

page 159

COOKBOOKS TO AVOID

CLASSIC New England Boiled Desserts

PASTA ON THE GRILL

HEADCHEESE HEADCHEESE HEADCHEESE at the Gilmore Inn

Technique de Manifold

page 219

"...because I'm more comfortable using my own tools. Now- how much longer do you want me to sand the minestrone?"

page 5

Cartoon Information:
Fax: 978-546-7747
E-Mail: richtennant@the5thwave.com
World Wide Web: www.the5thwave.com

Recipes at a Glance

Cream Soups

Meat and Poultry Soups

Fish and Seafood Soups

International Soups

Chilled Soups

Garnishes

Table of Contents

Introduction

● ●

Soup has long been recognized as a nutritious food that comforts and restores both body and soul. A pot of simmering soup on the stove typifies the warmth of home and hearth. It makes us feel good. Yet soup has not always been the symbol of home cooking. The first restaurants were located in Paris (but of course!) in the late 1700s and only served warming and hearty soups that even then were believed to have restorative powers. The word restaurant itself is derived from the French word *restaurer,* meaning to restore and refresh.

In this book, you'll find updated recipes for delicious classic, ethnic, and innovative soups. Make a batch — and regenerate, renew, and restore yourself, your family and friends.

How to Use This Book

Soup is one of the world's most versatile foods and offers endless possibilities. There are soups to accommodate different ethnic and regional tastes, texture preferences, and weather changes. No matter what you're looking for — light and delicate; warming and robust; smooth and creamy; or cool and refreshing — you'll find them all in this book. The good news is they're generally inexpensive and easy to make. No kidding.

The recipes range from healthier renditions of traditional favorites to delicious, ethnic specialties to sensational new soups. The book takes a realistic approach to modern cooking — because modern cooks don't always have the time! It gives you shortcuts that still produce great results. Your taste buds will swear that you've followed a lengthier, classic preparation.

You'll also find out about equipment, ingredients, and how-to techniques. There's even a chapter on substitutions and improvisation so you can put your own imprint on the recipes. With this arsenal of knowledge, you'll gain the confidence to make any recipe, even devise one of your own. You'll discover that making soup is easy and rewarding, and you end up with a great meal. Have fun!

What I Assume about You

You don't need to have any prior cooking knowledge to use this book. All of the recipes and ingredients are fully explained, as are general cooking concepts that pop up here and there. If you can boil water, you can make soup. No kidding. Just make sure that you have the right equipment as described in the first few chapters and you'll be making soup in no time.

If you happen to know a lot about cooking, you'll still find this book to be incredibly useful; not only for the recipes but also for the tips and tricks I've peppered throughout the book.

How This Book Is Organized

This single-subject cookbook is divided into six parts that'll guide you through all the aspects of soup preparation. It's filled with down-to-earth advice and fascinating information as well as obvious and not so obvious cooking tips. The book travels full circle, beginning in your kitchen, then heading out to the market, then into your kitchen where you can cook and finally to your table where you can savor the delectable homemade soups of many cultures. But feel free to skip around. If you already have a well-stocked kitchen and pantry, you can probably skim some of the early chapters in the book. Or if you just want to look up the recipe for, say, French Onion Soup, you can find it in the Index or the Recipes at a Glance and get cooking.

Many of the recipes are very easy to make, although a few are more challenging. The level of ease or difficulty, ballpark preparation and cooking times, special equipment needs such as a food processor or blender, and whether a certain soup is freezer worthy are indicated with each recipe.

Part 1: The Soup Kitchen

In this section, you'll find practical suggestions on setting up your kitchen so that you'll know what are the essential cooking tools and which staple food items to keep on hand. You'll have what you need, but you won't waste space or money on things you don't.

Part II: Souper Chef

This is the essence of soup cookery. I cover *mise en place* (how to set up before starting cooking), cooking techniques, what broth to use (including how to make your own), as well as food safety procedures. The final chapter in this part explains how to substitute ingredients and improvise so can you lend your individual touch to a recipe or make your own "signature soup."

Part III: Alphabet Soup

Here's your formal introduction to the building blocks of soup: the ingredients — from veggies to dairy, meat, poultry, and seafood. Although you might be familiar with some, others might be new to you. I show you how to use them in soups, which can be different compared to other preparations. Each chapter presents a wide selection of soup recipes featuring its highlighted ingredients. You're bound to find a few favorites among them.

Part IV: Souping Up

This part of the book shows you how to use seasonings — herbs and spices and the flavorings that make the recipes and your soup especially tasty. You'll find out the secrets of ethnic ingredient combinations and mild and spicy recipes from around the globe. The final chapter chills you out from your whirlwind world tour with recipes for cold soups.

Part V: From the Ladle to the Table

This section offers advice on how to serve soup, from menu hints, to what bowls to use, to garnishes. You'll be serving like a pro.

Part VI: The Part of Tens

Every *For Dummies* book ends with top-ten lists, and this one is no exception. I give you ten ways to correct soup mistakes and ten ideas for pairing soups with other courses in your meals.

Icons Used in This Book

Look for these icons next to tidbits of useful information:

When you see this icon, expect to find interesting tidbits, lore, and information about a particular soup, ingredient, or piece of equipment.

I place this icons next to information that will help you prevent mistakes or warn you against doing things that may potentially cause a problem.

Here you'll find culinary tips and common sense hints to make your cooking easier, more productive, and enjoyable.

I use this icon when I want you to, um, remember a general concept.

Part I
The Soup Kitchen

The 5th Wave   By Rich Tennant

"...because I'm more comfortable using my own tools. Now-how much longer do you want me to sand the minestrone?"

In this part . . .

Your kitchen is your culinary laboratory, and like any work space, it needs to be set up properly. In this part, you'll discover how to outfit your kitchen with equipment that's not only great for making soup but also can do double duty and be used to prepare many other meals. Kitchenware is an investment. You don't need lots of specialized tools, but a few quality items that will see you through. You'll also find out what food to keep in stock — on your shelves as well as in your fridge and freezer. Having a well-equipped kitchen will make a tremendous difference in how you cook and perhaps even how often.

Chapter 1

Tooling Up

*H*aving the right tools makes the time you spend in the kitchen more effective and efficient, but with the abundance of kitchen products on the market, how do you know exactly what you need? Before buying, ask yourself a few questions: Do I really need this? Will I use it? Is it well made? Will it last?

Soup doesn't require much equipment — on the most basic level, you'll need a good knife, a cutting board, a large pot with a lid, a wooden spoon, a ladle, and maybe an old-fashioned food-mill for purees. Those are the tools our grandmothers used, and they work well. Modern cooks have more choices, and several items make cooking easier and more enjoyable.

Pots and Pans

Pots and pans don't need to be expensive, but they should be well-made. Select those with tight-fitting lids and ovenproof handles that are securely attached with rivets, screws, or sturdy welding. Soup pots should be a medium- to heavy-gauge metal with a thick bottom, so that the heat stays evenly distributed and foods don't scorch. Thin-bottomed pots warp more easily and get hot spots where food invariably burns no matter how low the heat source. Make sure that you'll be able to comfortably lift the pot even when it's filled with soup. Pots can last a lifetime, so consider your options and buy the best quality within your budget.

Stock pots and dutch ovens: What gives?

Stock pots are tall and narrow with straight sides and are used for making stock or broth. Dutch ovens are shorter and wider, sometimes with slightly curved sides and are perfect for making soups and stews. You can also use them to make smaller batches of broth.

You need these items as your basic setup (some of which are shown in Figure 1-1):

- 4½- to 6-quart heavy Dutch oven with lid
- 1½-quart saucepan with lid
- 2½- to 3-quart saucepan with lid
- 10-inch skillet (the Dutch oven's lid may fit)
- 8- to 10-quart stock pot with lid (optional)

Figure 1-1: You need these pots if you're going to make soup.

The best choices are enameled cast iron, stainless steel with an aluminum core or thick aluminum bottom, and medium- to heavy-weight enameled pots, because they retain heat well. Aluminum, although an excellent heat conductor, reacts with food, particularly acidic foods such as tomatoes, and can impart a metallic taste if food is left in the pot too long after cooking. Anodized aluminum pots are a medium gray color and have been treated to react less with food. Plain cast iron needs to be well seasoned to prevent rusting. It, too, can react slightly with acidic foods.

Nonstick surfaces help you reduce the amount of fat you use, and pans with such surfaces can be ideal for some people. However, if the coating is cracked, flaking, or peeling, don't use the pot. Replace it.

Knives

A sharp knife is a cook's best friend. You'll need only three to four knives, and — as with other kitchen tools — if you buy good quality, knives should last for years. Ideally, the blade should be high-carbon stainless steel, because the edge stays sharp longer than ordinary stainless steel. Knives should feel good in your hand and not be too big or unwieldy. Follow your gut instinct on this one, not a friend's or salesperson's recommendation. Knives should be well-balanced and have handles that are securely riveted or attached. Store them in a knife block or on a knife rack so they'll stay sharp. If you toss them in a drawer, they become dull more quickly.

You need these items to begin your knife collection (see Figure 1-2):

- 3- to 4-inch paring knife
- 6- to 8-inch chef's knife for chopping
- Serrated knife for slicing bread and tomatoes
- 8- to 10-inch slicing knife (optional)
- Carving or large kitchen fork
- Sharpening steel
- Sharpening stone or knife sharpener

Figure 1-2:
Just a few of the knife-related items you need.

You must care for your knives. To do this effectively, you need both a sharpening stone or an electric or nonelectric sharpening machine, as well as a sharpening steel. A steel straightens the edge of the knife, but doesn't actually sharpen it. Try to use the steel at least once or twice a week. If your knife is only a bit dull, the edge probably isn't straight. Often, a few strokes on a steel can restore it. Once a month you should sharpen your knives, and then pass them on the steel. Serrated knives don't need to be maintained this way. If a serrated blade no longer cuts well, it should be replaced.

If you're unsure how to use any of the cutlery or sharpening equipment, ask the salesperson at a cookware shop or a knowledgeable friend to demonstrate the proper technique. Have her watch you do it so she can guide you. Learning to use these instruments correctly and safely is important. I know this sounds easy, and it is. How-to drawings in books or magazines can give you the proper idea, but nothing's better than actually watching someone with skill and repeating her action.

Cuts happen more often with dull knives because you have to work harder and exert more pressure on the blade in order to slice or chop properly. A sharp knife requires less effort on your part. Let a sharp blade do more of the work for you.

Essential Utensils

You'll find zillions of gadgets and utensils on the market. Some are excellent, timesaving tools, but many are expensive fads — things that you'll use a few times and never again.

Basic equipment

You need the following items to begin building the foundation of your cooking arena:

- ✔ Baking sheet
- ✔ Can and bottle opener
- ✔ Colander
- ✔ Cooling rack
- ✔ Cutting boards
- ✔ Grater, preferably four-sided
- ✔ Measuring cup set, for both dry and liquid ingredients
- ✔ Measuring spoons
- ✔ Mixing bowls
- ✔ Sieves (medium diameter, one fine mesh and one medium mesh)

Keeping your cutting board safe

To minimize the risk of contamination, have more than one cutting board — one for vegetables, fruit, garlic, ginger, and herbs, and the other for meat, poultry, and fish. A separate wooden board is ideal for baked goods. Experts disagree which material, plastic or wood, is most sanitary, but whatever you choose, keep the boards clean. Wash, but don't soak, the boards in hot soapy water. Antibacterial dish detergents are a good choice. You can also rub kosher or coarse salt on the board before washing to remove any particles caught in tiny grooves that are invisible to your eye. Plastic boards can go in the dishwasher.

- ✔ Storage containers for freezer and refrigerator with covers and/or self-sealing plastic storage bags
- ✔ Ladle
- ✔ Skimmer
- ✔ Spoons (wooden, slotted, and solid)
- ✔ Tongs
- ✔ Vegetable peeler
- ✔ Wine opener

In addition to these items, you'll need a supply of aluminum foil, freezer paper, paper towels, and plastic wrap.

To keep cutting boards from slipping on your countertop, place a damp paper towel underneath the board.

Hand and Electric Appliances

You don't need many appliances for cooking, but your soup kitchen will be complete if you own one or two of these handy tools. Buy what you'll actually use on a fairly regular basis or items that you honestly think you can't do without.

Hand or immersion blender

A hand or immersion blender is a wonderful appliance. One is shown in Figure 1-3. It's convenient, portable, and very easy to use. Plug it in, immerse the blades into the food you want to puree, and switch on the power. Move the blender around the pot until the desired texture is achieved. You can create a chunky consistency by pureeing partially or one that's fine and smooth by pureeing completely. Sometimes, a few chunks of food escape the blades. You might want to "feel" for them by slowly stirring the soup with a wooden spoon, and then using the hand blender again in that area. Vegetables must be very soft for a hand blender to perform at its best. Clean up is a breeze — wash the blades in soapy water and rinse.

Food processor

The modern kitchen's workhorse, a food processor can be used for everything from making pastry to shredding cabbage. Fitted with the steel blade, it is good for pureeing thick soups, as well as for chopping onions. The texture it produces is not as smooth as what you'll get with a blender or hand blender. To compensate, you might want to strain the solid ingredients and puree them in batches with a little of the broth, and then combine them afterward. The end result definitely will have a finer texture.

When using a food processor, don't overfill the bowl. It can leak from the top and bottom. It's best to puree in small batches and fill the bowl about one-third to one-half full. Pulse several times until the puree forms.

Blender

This all-around tool has been on the market for years. It is fine for fairly thin pureed soups such as carrot or tomato, but it doesn't work as well for thicker purees such as beans or lentils. If you use a blender, always puree in batches, filling the container only one-third full. Start the blender at a low speed, and then while it's running, adjust it to a higher level. If it's too full, the soup will leak out. And if the soup's hot, you can get burned.

Food mill

Grandma's forerunner to the food processor, this nonelectric tool often has interchangeable discs that can be used for shredding as well as pureeing to various textures, depending on which blade you use (see Figure 1-3). If you want to use it for purees for soups, the vegetables must be very soft. Food mills both puree and strain simultaneously, taking out skins and undercooked vegetables, as well as seeds, making it a good choice for tomato and berry purees.

HAND BLENDER

FOOD MILL

Figure 1-3:
A hand
blender and
a food mill.

Spice mill

Hand spice mills look similar to large pepper mills with a crankshaft and an opening on top to load the whole spices and a container below to catch the ground spices. They're easy to use and can be found in good cookware shops. If you prefer to use an electric spice mill, choose a small, inexpensive coffee grinder that you earmark for spices only. Partially fill the container with spices, turn on the power, and in a matter of seconds, they are freshly ground.

Chapter 2

Stocking Up

- -

In This Chapter

▶ Learning the basic items to keep on your shelves

▶ Knowing what to have on hand in your refrigerator and freezer

▶ Remembering what spices, herbs, and condiments you should stock

- -

*H*aving a variety of ingredients at home makes cooking easier. It also gives you greater flexibility and can spark your culinary imagination. Sometimes, you'll already have everything you need to start cooking right away, so you won't have to dash out and shop.

Supply your kitchen with foods that you like and use often, of course, but add a few exotic spices, condiments, or ethnic ingredients. You don't need to keep more than one or two of each item on your shelves unless you cook with it regularly, such as canned tomatoes or broth. It's helpful to keep a grocery list handy in your kitchen so you can mark down if you need to replace any staples that you've used.

In Your Kitchen Cabinets

Years ago, items with a long shelf-life were stored in a separate pantry that was located off the kitchen. Few of us have pantries anymore. Instead, we keep these items in our kitchen cupboards.

You need to keep these staples on hand so you'll be ready for almost anything:

✔ Apple juice

✔ Barley, pearled

✔ Beans (assorted dried and canned)

✔ Broth, low-sodium chicken and beef

✔ Clams, canned

✔ Clam juice

- Crackers
- Flour, all-purpose
- Lentils, brown
- Mussels, canned or bottled
- Olive oil
- Pasta, assorted shapes
- Peanut butter, natural style
- Rice (white, basmati, brown, and wild)
- Salmon, canned
- Salad dressing
- Sugar (white and brown)
- Tomatoes (assorted canned varieties: whole plum, chopped, pureed)
- Tomato paste, preferably small cans or resealable tube
- Vegetable oil (such as peanut, safflower, or corn)

In a Cool, Dry Place

You'll use most of these staples almost every day, but a few might be reserved for special recipes. Except for dried mushrooms, which I keep in a self-sealing plastic bag, I like to keep the following items in a fairly dark spot where some air circulates around them so they don't spoil or grow sprouts as quickly. These items can be stored in a basket, cabinet, or drawer:

- Garlic
- Mushrooms, dried (such as shiitake or porcini)
- Onions
- Potatoes
- Sweet potatoes
- Winter squash (such as butternut or acorn)

In Your Fridge

You won't need every one of the dairy and produce items listed here, but this section notes what's helpful to have at your fingertips. If the item is something I don't use often, such as Half-and-Half, cream, buttermilk, or highly perishable items, I buy it when called for in a recipe. The same goes for most fragile, fresh produce such as mushrooms, lettuce, green beans, spinach, and the like. Although parsley and lemons don't last long, they're so versatile and used so often for both flavoring and garnishing in everything from soups to salads to entrees, I suggest e always having them on hand.

- ✔ Butter or margarine
- ✔ Eggs
- ✔ Milk (low-fat or 2%)
- ✔ Sour cream (regular or nonfat)
- ✔ Yogurt, preferably low-fat
- ✔ Apples
- ✔ Carrots
- ✔ Celery
- ✔ Bell peppers
- ✔ Ginger, fresh (a 2- to 3-inch piece)
- ✔ Lemons
- ✔ Oranges
- ✔ Parsley
- ✔ Scallions

You can freeze butter or margarine for several months. Wrap it well in plastic wrap or put it in a self-sealing bag so it doesn't develop freezer burn, which affects its taste.

In Your Freezer

If you have a small freezer, keep on hand only what you think you'll use in a month or so. If you have a large freezer compartment or a separate appliance, keep a good supply of ingredients at your disposal. Make sure meat and seafood are wrapped in freezer paper or wrapped well and put in freezer bags before freezing. The vegetables listed below are packaged frozen products.

You need these items to have a well-stocked freezer:

- ✔ Beef bottom round or chuck, cubed
- ✔ Bread or rolls
- ✔ Broccoli or cauliflower florets

- Corn kernels
- Chicken parts or boneless chicken pieces
- Green beans
- Lima beans
- Oxtail
- Peas
- Shrimp
- Spinach, chopped or whole

Seasoning

Cooks commonly use an array of seasonings from around the world. Your cabinet will reflect the diversity of your personal culinary taste. Don't rush out and fill the spice rack. Buy what you use frequently; otherwise, buy spices as you need them for specific recipes. You'll need these flavorful ingredients for the soup recipes in this book.

Spices

These ingredients will really spice up your soups:

- Allspice (whole berries and ground)
- Caraway seeds
- Cardamom (whole and ground)
- Cayenne or ground red chili pepper
- Cloves (whole and ground)
- Chili powder
- Crushed red chili flakes
- Cinnamon (sticks and ground)
- Coriander (ground or whole)
- Cumin (ground)
- Curry powder, preferably Madras style

✔ Mustard, dried English style

✔ Nutmeg, preferably whole so it can be freshly grated, on the small side of a grater; otherwise, ground

✔ Paprika and/or Hungarian sweet paprika

✔ Black peppercorns (to be freshly ground)

✔ White pepper (ground or white peppercorns if you have a mill specifically for white pepper)

✔ Turmeric

Herbs

These ingredients are just waiting for the chance to flavor your soups:

✔ Basil

✔ Bay leaf

✔ Chives

✔ Cilantro, fresh

✔ Dill, fresh

✔ Mint, fresh

✔ Oregano

✔ Parsley, fresh (preferably flat-leaf)

✔ Rosemary

✔ Thyme leaves

Significant others

These ingredients will add well-known and not-so-well-known flavors to your soups:

✔ Dijon mustard

✔ Chinese sesame oil

✔ Chinese chili oil

✔ Salt (kosher, fine-grained, or sea salt)

- ✔ Sherry
- ✔ Soy sauce
- ✔ Tabasco or other liquid hot red pepper sauce
- ✔ Thai fish sauce
- ✔ Vermouth, dry white
- ✔ Wine vinegar, rice wine, and/or white wine
- ✔ Worcestershire sauce

Seal spices, herbs, and condiments after opening to keep them fresh. Check condiment labels to see if they need to be refrigerated after opening.

Part II
Souper Chef

The 5th Wave   By Rich Tennant

"Oooo, what's in here? Is that sun-dried eye of newt? How gourmet!"

In this part . . .

When it's time to make a meal, having a workable game plan is key. You, the cook, need a strategy from start to finish. The chapters in this part give you the know-how needed to get from reading recipes to embarking on a sane shopping trip for the items you need in your kitchen.

You'll discover all the processes, beginning with organizing your initial preparations, a commonsense procedure called *mise en place* that makes the whole cooking experience more pleasurable. You'll also get the inside scoop on what techniques are commonly used in making soup, when and where to apply them, as well as advice on how to cook and store food safely. There's even a chapter on improvising that will give you the confidence to experiment and create some of your own chef d'oeuvres.

Chapter 3

Ready . . . Set . . . Soup!

*Y*ou've browsed through recipes and decided on one that appeals to you and that you have both the time and the inclination to prepare. This chapter provides pointers to guide you through the cooking process.

Getting Started

The first step is to check your own stock before heading out to shop. As obvious as this seems, it's annoying to have to make a second trip because you thought you had an ingredient, but you don't, or to end up with four bottles of ground cinnamon on your shelf because you did have it already. Do you have a blender? Don't you have a bag of apples in the garage? Are the onions still fresh? Just how old is that curry powder hidden behind the box of salt? Should it be thrown out and replaced?

After you've finished your inventory, make a shopping list. It's easiest if you group the items by category, the way you're likely to find them in the store: as produce, dairy, meat, canned goods, spices, and so on. This way, you won't do as much backtracking from aisle to aisle. Wherever you head off to do the grocery shopping — to a supermarket, green grocer, butcher, or fish shop — make sure it's a place where the quality is consistently good for a reasonable price.

When shopping, select canned and staple items first, and then choose produce, refrigerated meat, poultry, and seafood, and finally put frozen items into your basket.

Souper Preparations

After shopping, read the recipe again thoroughly so you know what you need to do. Then the time has come to round up everything required to make your chosen recipe. Chefs call this activity "*mise en place*," a French phrase that means "put in place." Professional cooks colloquially shorten the phrase and refer to this as their *place*.

To begin, you'll need to gather all the equipment — pots, pans, measuring spoons and cups, blenders, sieves, skimmers, and utensils. Keep them handy so you don't have to root through drawers and cabinets after you've started cooking. Having these items available prevents you from panicking or burning food that's already in progress. In addition to equipment, you must lay out all the ingredients you'll use.

To complete your *place,* you'll have to prep the ingredients, which includes measuring, cutting, and precooking. After everything is ready (see Figure 3-1), only then should you begin to make the recipe. This practical process helps to ensure a successful outcome, whether you're making a simple soup or the most elegant pastry.

MISE EN PLACE

Figure 3-1:
Each in its
own place.

Delicate items such as seafood, poultry, and meat can be kept in the fridge until you're ready to prep them. You may want to cover them loosely and return them to the fridge if you're not going to use them within 15 to 30 minutes, so they don't have a chance to spoil.

Don't measure herbs and spices over the pot. Sometimes, too much of an ingredient flows out at once and goes into the soup. Instead, measure herbs and spices over the counter or into a small dish and set them aside to add at the appropriate time.

Prep It

How you prep an item for cooking can determine the result. Follow both the recipe instructions and these guidelines.

It's in the cut

To make your time in the kitchen easier and faster, familiarize yourself with the terms and the different cutting methods used in recipes, and take a look at Figure 3-2. And make sure you're your knife is sharp before you begin:

- **Chop:** To cut food into irregular pieces that are ¼ inch to ½ inch in diameter. Vegetables such as onions, carrots, celery, and tomatoes are often chopped.

- **Cube:** To cut food into fairly uniform squares, from ½ inch up to 2 inches as indicated in the recipe. Meats are often cubed, as well as large vegetables such as eggplant and butternut squash.

- **Dice:** To cut food, such as onions, into uniformly shaped pieces ¼ inch to ½ inch. This is basically a smaller cube and is used primarily for vegetables, to give the finished dish a more polished look.

- **Mince:** To cut into small pieces less than ⅛ inch. It's the smallest cut and helps release flavors in aromatic foods. It is primarily used for garlic, ginger, shallots, and fresh herbs.

- **Shred:** To cut into relatively thin, but irregular strips. This is generally done on a grater, and the side of the grater that's used determines how thick the shreds will be. Cabbage and carrots are usually done on the largest holes, whereas harder or aromatic items such as Parmesan and Romano cheese, lemon zest, or fresh ginger are grated on smaller holes. Some foods — such as lettuce, spinach, and cabbage — can also be shredded by slicing them very thinly.

- ✔ **Slice:** To cut food into pieces of uniform thickness.

- ✔ **Very thinly slice:** To cut food into uniformly thin pieces about ⅛ inch thick or less.

- ✔ **Slice in very thin strips:** To cut food into uniformly thin strips or matchsticks about ⅛ inch thick. This cut is also known as julienne or matchstick and is often used for vegetables such as cucumber, carrot, zucchini, and yellow squash.

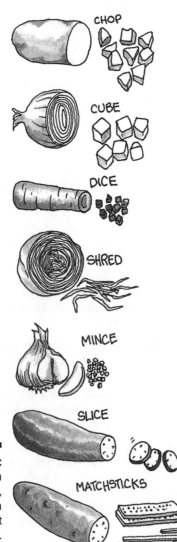

CHOP

CUBE

DICE

SHRED

MINCE

SLICE

MATCHSTICKS

Figure 3-2:
You can slice, dice, chop, and a whole lot more.

Whether you're chopping, dicing, mincing, or slicing, cut each raw ingredient into pieces of similar size. You don't have to measure anything with a ruler; just judge the size with your eyes. If you cut one ingredient into varying sizes, each piece would have a different cooking time. During the cooking process, some would already be tender while others would still be tough.

Suppose that a soup calls for sliced carrots, cubed potatoes, shredded cabbage, and beef cut into 1-inch cubes. The carrots should be basically the same length or width and the potatoes cubed to a size similar as the carrots. All the cabbage should be shredded to the same thickness. The beef should be cubed to relatively the same shape and size. This is especially important for vegetables with the same texture, such as carrots, potatoes, and parsnips, so they finish simultaneously.

Keep prepped ingredients separate until you are ready to use them. You can put them in individual bowls, in disposable plastic bags, or in piles on a baking sheet or cutting board. You may want to cover cut vegetables with a damp paper towel to prevent them from withering.

Measuring Up

You may not think that measuring ingredients is important. After all, chefs on television cooking shows just fling a bit of this and some of that into the pot, and the recipe works out great. Keep three things in mind: (1) Nobody is going to eat that television food, which is possibly misted with lots of vegetable oil or sprayed with unnamable chemicals to give it the right look under the lights, (2) more than likely, the TV chef is experienced, and experience allows anyone, including you, to have freer rein, and (3) behind the scenes there's a kitchen staff who have prepped the ingredients for the star. Imagine what you would end up with if you didn't measure correctly and added 2 tablespoons of curry and ½ teaspoon of cayenne when all you needed was 2 teaspoons of curry and a ¼ teaspoon of cayenne? Not the end of the world, but probably far too spicy. (To repair this, you could make another batch of the recipe, very lightly spiced, and combine the two.) Suppose that you add 3½ cups of broth instead of 2½ cups? Perhaps the soup will be too thin. Sometimes, these mistakes work out, but if you're a beginning cook, that's not always the case. It's good to know how and what to measure so you have a better chance of getting consistently good results, even if you feel like experimenting in your kitchen lab.

Measures come in both dry and liquid cups. Wet and dry measuring cups aren't interchangeable, and you'll need both in order to do the job accurately. Fortunately, cooking is far more forgiving of sloppy measuring — something we're all prone to when we're in a hurry — than is baking.

✔ **Glass and clear plastic measuring cups are used for liquids (see Figure 3-3).** They generally come in 1-, 2-, and 4-cup measures. Set the measure on the countertop, and pour in the ingredient. Bend over to check it at eye level, and make sure that the liquid rises to the correct line. For larger amounts, there are 2- and 3-quart plastic bowls with a handle and a spout that is convenient for pouring liquid.

✔ **Dry measuring cups are made of stainless steel, aluminum, or plastic (see Figure 3-4).** They come in sets of ¼-, ⅓-, ½-, and 1-cup sizes, although occasionally you can get a ⅛-cup (a coffee measure) or a 2-cup measure as well. Spoon the dry ingredients into the cup — don't dip the cup into an ingredient — and then level off the top with the flat side of a knife or spatula to get an accurate measure. Although measuring in this way is not as important with things like chopped vegetables, fruit, or nuts, using this method is crucial for flour and other dry ingredients.

✔ **Measuring spoon sets are made of stainless steel, aluminum, or plastic (see Figure 3-5).** They are also graded from ¼ teaspoon, ½ teaspoon, 1 teaspoon, and 1 tablespoon. Some sets also include a ½-tablespoon measure, which is equivalent to 1½ teaspoons. Measuring ⅛ teaspoon is easy: Just fill a ¼-teaspoon measure halfway. A "pinch" or a "dash" is less than ⅛ teaspoon. When measuring ingredients with spoons, try to keep the ingredients level to the top, neither lower than the top nor heaping over it. This makes quite a difference when measuring spices.

LIQUID MEASURE

Figure 3-3:
A clear measuring cup for liquids.

DRY MEASURE

Figure 3-4:
Measuring cups for dry ingredients.

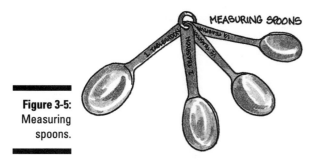

MEASURING SPOONS

Figure 3-5:
Measuring
spoons.

Get Cooking!

Your *mise en place* is all set. Remember to read the recipe again before you actually begin cooking to reacquaint yourself with all the steps and their proper sequence. Take a moment to get it clear in your mind, and make a few notes if you feel so inclined. Keep the recipe nearby as a handy reference.

Chapter 4

Soup Techniques

● ●

In This Chapter

▶ Knowing when to use the different kinds of broth

▶ Knowing when to sauté vegetables — and when not to

● ●

*A*ll soups aren't made alike. Sometimes, ingredients are sautéed first; other times, everything's put into the pot at once. Some soups are made with broth, others with water. What's consistent is that soup and broth should be gently simmered, and never boiled. Boiling returns any impurities, such as fat or foam that has risen to the surface, back into the soup. It also makes proteins like meat stringier or tougher, and boiling can evaporate too much of the liquid, letting solid ingredients scorch or stick to the bottom of the pot. Although soup or broth may be brought up to a boil, the heat should then be reduced so the liquid simmers or bubbles gently. The pot is to be covered, partially covered, or left uncovered as the recipes indicate.

Broth Origins: Homemade, Canned, and Instant

There's nothing like homemade broth. It's wholesome and rich tasting, and it's the substructure of many wonderful soups. You'll find recipes for several standard broths in Chapter 5 that you will generally use whenever you want homemade taste.

Broth is made by simmering water with the flesh and bones of poultry, meat, and fish along with a few vegetables. You can also make broth simply by simmering a combination of vegetables. The liquid is strained and which becomes the base for various soups. In the traditional definition, stocks are generally prepared from just bones (with no flesh) and vegetable trimmings. For the purposes of most cookbooks and recipes for the home cook, the words broth and stock usually refer to the same thing — a flavored liquid made from poultry, fish, or meat and/or vegetables.

Meat, poultry, and fish broth should have a minimum of seasoning, such as a few herbs or a bouquet garni, or contain aromatic vegetables, such as carrots, celery, onions, or leeks, but the broth should never be salted. Some cooks like to add salt while cooking vegetable broth, but I think it's wiser to wait and add salt at the end of a soup recipe.

Make a batch of broth and freeze it so you'll always have it on hand when you need it.

Homemade broth rules

You'll want to follow these simple rules when making broth from scratch:

- ✔ Always start with cold water.
- ✔ For the most flavor, the water should cover the solid ingredients by a few inches. If the water is too deep, the broth will be thin and flavorless.
- ✔ Simmer, don't boil. At the onset, you can bring the water to a boil, then reduce the temperature so the liquid simmers as it turns into broth.
- ✔ Skim off fat and foam from the surface during the cooking process. Use a ladle or skimmer. You can also use a skimmer or slotted spoon to remove whole spices and herbs.
- ✔ If the broth is too bland, simmer it a bit longer to reduce it and concentrate the flavor.
- ✔ If it's too strong, add extra water.
- ✔ Strain the broth through a fine-meshed sieve. Do not press on the ingredients in the sieve. (The only exception is vegetable stock: To extract the greatest degree of vegetable flavor, press the vegetables in the sieve gently with the back of a spoon.)
- ✔ Use broth immediately or chill it quickly, and then refrigerate it.
- ✔ Remove fat from finished broth by chilling it or by using a gravy separator.

Canned and instant broth

In all honesty, I don't always have time to make homemade broth. Sometimes, I feel like making soup and don't have the time or the inclination to thaw what's in my freezer. For convenience, I use prepared broth. Some supermarkets sell "freshly made" chicken broth that they keep refrigerated or frozen, and it's almost as good as homemade.

Like many other people with busy lives, I often use canned broth. Try to purchase low-sodium versions that are available in the soup aisle or in health food or diet sections of supermarkets. Although they are less salty than the regular versions, they still tend to be far more salty than homemade, so the soup you make with them won't need much additional salt, if any.

Bouillon cubes and powders are notoriously high in sodium and should be used only if nothing else is available. Although some higher quality cubes are sold in health food stores, most bouillon cubes lack the depth of flavor found in homemade, or even in canned, broth.

I rarely salt any soup that I've made with bouillon. To cut the salt, I may alter the ratio of cubes to water, using one cup more of water per cube than the amount indicated on the package. The vegetables or meat in the soup create additional flavor and make up for using fewer cubes. Whatever type of broth you end up using — homemade, canned, or bouillon — pay attention to the saltiness of the broth and use caution so that your finished soup doesn't become too salty to eat.

Eliminate excess fat in homemade broth and soup by cooling it to lukewarm and refrigerating it for several hours or overnight. The fat will solidify on the surface and can be removed easily.

Basic Techniques: To Sauté or Not to Sauté

Sauté is a French word that literally means to jump, but it also refers to a fundamental cooking process. To sauté, place a pot over medium heat, and melt butter or margarine or heat a small amount of vegetable or olive oil. Add the ingredients and cook, stirring vegetables occasionally or turning meat only once or twice. Don't overcrowd the pan or the food will steam.

Many well-prepared soups start with a quick sauté of aromatic vegetables — onions, leeks, carrots, celery, or scallions. Sautéing helps to release the full taste and the natural sugars in the vegetables. Fragrant flavor enhancers such as garlic, ginger, chilis, lemon grass, or spices that require cooking to unlock their taste are most often added after the aromatic vegetables begin to soften. These sautéed ingredients create a delicious layer of flavor for the soup. This preparation method is often used in pureed soups, as well as in some vegetable and poultry soups.

The veggie foundation of most soups

Did you know that a term exists for the combination of chopped aromatic vegetables, such as onions, celery, and carrots, found in many soups and sauces? The French call it *mirepoix*, the Spanish call it *sofrito* (and they add pork fat and annatto seeds, for a red color), and Italians call it *soffrito* (they tend to add green peppers). Sometimes, garlic is added after a few minutes. Sometimes, the carrots are omitted and leeks are added. Creole and Cajun cooking uses a combination of onion, scallions, and green bell peppers.

After sautéing, add the wet ingredients such as tomatoes, wine, broth, or other liquid to the pot. Other ingredients, such as vegetables, pasta, rice, or proteins, are added, and the liquid is brought up to a boil. The heat is then reduced so that the soup simmers gently until it is finished.

You'll also find recipes in which ingredients are combined in the pot with liquid without sautéing at all. Again, the liquid is brought to a boil and the heat is reduced so that the soup simmers. It's a different kind of culinary brew, but equally tasty. You may find this process used more often in some hearty ethnic soups, such as those based on legumes.

Seasoning Soups with Whole Herbs and Spices

Many recipes call for whole spices or herbs that can be removed by the cook or the diner. Some cultures consider it to be good luck when a portion contains a whole spice. If you prefer not to serve whole spices or herbs in your soup, you can remove them with a slotted spoon or use a small fine mesh strainer or skimmer to remove them.

Another way to handle whole spices is to make a bouquet garni by wrapping the whole herbs or spices in a small piece of cheesecloth or in the rinsed leaf of a leek, and tie it securely before adding it to the pot. Remove the bouquet garni before serving. In a pinch you can put the herbs in a small metal tea ball and add it into the broth. Sometimes, whole herbs or spices are sautéed with vegetables, before the addition of broth, to bring out their fullest flavor. After sautéing, remove them with a slotted spoon and wrap them in cheesecloth and return the sack to the pot with the broth.

Salting Soups

When making broth, soup, and stews or any long-simmering item, don't salt the food until near or at the end of the cooking time. Some of the liquid always evaporates and gauging precisely the final intensity of the salt in the soup is difficult. If you use canned broth, it already contains salt, which will become stronger as the soup simmers. If you salt at the beginning, the salt taste will become more potent, and you'll end up with soup that's over-seasoned.

You'll notice that the recipes in this book don't specify the amount of salt, but make a suggestion. This isn't an oversight or a trick. I don't know whether you're using homemade, regular canned, low-sodium canned, or cubed broth, which all have different sodium contents. Taste the soup at the end; add the salt in small amounts. You can always add more but you can't take it out after it's in.

Most soups will require between ½ to 1 teaspoon of salt, but taste first!

Chapter 5

Liquid Foundations

In This Chapter

▶ Creating homemade broth
▶ Making richer-tasting browned broths

*T*asty on its own, a good broth is the basis for a great soup, as well as stews and sauces. It's not difficult to make, but it requires time. Unlike commercially processed, canned broths or bouillon cubes, the broth recipes in this book are salt-free. When making soup with homemade broth, adjust the salt to your taste. After the broth is made, strain it with a fine mesh sieve or a medium sieve lined with cheesecloth. Broth kept longer than two to three days must be frozen or brought back to a vigorous boil and chilled again. It will then last for another 2 to 3 days in the refrigerator. If storing broth, chill according to the directions in Chapter 6.

Meat and Poultry Broth

These classic meat and poultry broth recipes run the gamut from traditional chicken and beef to more robust browned broths. Although they're generally considered the basis of most soups, I find a warm cup of homemade broth is also wonderful on its own.

Chicken Broth

I like to make lots of chicken broth at once and keep it in my freezer. If you prefer, make a smaller amount by cutting this recipe in half. Richer flavored Browned Chicken Broth appears later in this chapter.

Yield: *About 2½ quarts*

Level: *Easy to intermediate*

Cooking time: *3½ to 4½ hours*

Freezes well for 4 to 6 months

5 pounds chicken parts (necks, backs, thighs, and wings)

2 medium carrots, unpeeled and cut into chunks

1 medium onion, peeled and halved

3 celery stalks with leaves attached, cut into chunks

1½ teaspoons black peppercorns

1 bay leaf

4 sprigs parsley

4 to 5 quarts water or enough to cover

1 In a large stockpot, combine the chicken parts, carrots, onion, celery, peppercorns, bay leaf, and parsley. Add the water to cover.

2 Over medium-high heat, bring to a boil. Skim off any foam. After the liquid boils, reduce the heat to medium-low. Simmer for 3 to 4 hours, skimming the fat and foam every half hour or so. Add more water if too much has evaporated.

3 Strain the broth and discard the solids. Use the broth immediately or cool, uncovered, by placing the pot in an ice bath and stirring the broth,. Then refrigerate it for several hours or overnight and remove any solidified fat. Use within 2 to 3 days, or freeze.

Variation: *Turkey Soup: Use turkey parts or a meaty, cut-up, leftover carcass from a holiday meal and some of the leftover meat.*

Tip: *If your pot is too small to hold the full recipe, make less or divide the batch and cook in more than one pot.*

Per Serving: *Calories 29.1; Protein 0.5g; Carbohydrates 3.0g; Dietary fiber 0.8g; Total fat 1.8g; Saturated fat 0.5g; Cholesterol 1.5mg; Sodium 35.4mg.*

Beef Broth

Many recipes for beef broth require roasted bones and several time-consuming steps. This beef broth is easy to prepare, and the recipe can be doubled. Richer flavored Browned Beef Broth appears later in this chapter.

Yield: *About 2 quarts*

Level: *Easy to intermediate*

Cooking time: *2 to 2½ hours*

Freezes well for 4 to 6 months

2½ to 3 pounds beef bottom round or rump roast, cut into a few large chunks

2 medium carrots, cut into chunks

1 medium onion, peeled and halved

2 celery stalks with leaves attached, cut into chunks

2 plum tomatoes, halved and seeded

2 sprigs parsley

1 bay leaf

3½ to 4 quarts water

1 In a large stockpot, combine the beef, carrots, onion, celery, tomatoes, parsley, and bay leaf. Add the water to cover.

2 Over medium-high heat, bring to a boil. Skim off any foam. When the liquid boils, reduce the heat to medium-low and simmer for 1½ to 2 hours, skimming the fat and foam every half hour or so. Add more water if too much has evaporated.

3 Strain the broth and reserve the meat, but discard the remaining solid ingredients. The meat can be sliced and served. Use the broth immediately or cool, uncovered, by placing the pot in an ice bath and stirring the broth. Refrigerate it for several hours or overnight and remove any solidified fat. Use within 2 to 3 days or freeze.

Variation: *For a stronger-tasting chicken or beef broth, just reduce. Once strained and cooled, and the fat has been removed, return the broth to a saucepan and simmer over medium heat until the broth is reduced by half. This broth would be excellent in soups, stews, and sauces where you want a richer taste.*

Per Serving: *Calories 20.2; Protein 0.5g; Carbohydrates 2.0g; Dietary fiber 0.5g; Total fat 1.2g; Saturated fat 0.5g; Cholesterol 1.6mg; Sodium 18.1mg.*

Browned Chicken Broth

Yield: About 2½ quarts

Level: Easy to Intermediate

Time: 3½ to 4½ hours

Freezes well for 4 to 6 months

5 pounds chicken parts, (necks, backs, thighs, and wings)

2 medium carrots, unpeeled and cut into chunks

1 medium onion, peeled and halved

3 celery stalks with leaves attached, cut into chunks

4 to 5 quarts water or enough to cover

1½ teaspoons black peppercorns

1 bay leaf

4 sprigs parsley

1 Roast the bones and parts at 400 degrees F for 40 to 50 minutes or until lightly browned, turning them a few times during the roasting process and making sure that the bones don't burn. Add the vegetables after 20 minutes.

2 After the bones and veggies are browned, transfer them to a large soup or stock pot. Deglaze the roasting pan with water. Add the rich brown liquid to the pot.

3 Cover the meat or vegetables with water. Add the peppercorns, bay leaf, and parsley. Over medium-high heat, bring the liquid to a boil. Skim off any foam. After the liquid comes to a boil, reduce the heat to medium-low.

4 Simmer for 3 to 4 hours, skimming the fat and foam every half hour or so. Add additional water if too much has evaporated.

5 Strain the broth and discard the solids. Use immediately or cool by placing the pot, uncovered, in an ice bath and stirring the broth. Refrigerate it for several hours or overnight and remove any solidified fat. Use within 2 to 3 days or freeze.

Per Serving: Calories 36.0; Protein 0.4g; Carbohydrates 3.0g; Dietary fiber 0.8g; Total fat 2.6g; Saturated fat 0.8g; Cholesterol 2.2mg; Sodium 34.6mg.

Deglazing

To deglaze a roasting pan, pour 1 to 1½ cups hot or boiling water into the pan. Scrape the bottom with a wooden spoon to loosen any browned bits. Use this liquid in broth and sauces, strained or not, as indicated in the recipe.

Fancy browned or roasted broth

The term brown broth used to refer only to rich-tasting meat broth. The meaty bones and the vegetables used in the broth were roasted before being simmered to make the flavor deeper and fuller and to give it a dark, appetizing brown color. But brown broth doesn't have to include meat. You can make a roasted vegetable broth and a brown chicken broth in addition to the more traditional beef broth. Don't use this method for fish or shellfish broth, which should be light in color.

Roasted or browned broths take longer to make but have a more robust taste. After you've mastered the basic broth recipes or when you have extra time, you might want to try making one of these.

Browned Beef Broth

1 Follow the Browned Chicken Broth recipe in this chapter, but use 2½ pounds of chicken parts and 2½ pounds of meaty beef bones or oxtail.

2 Follow the instructions for Browned Chicken Broth, but roast for 45 minutes to 1 hour, adding the vegetables after 20 minutes. Continue to make the broth as directed.

Per Serving: Calories 34.2; Protein 0.6g; Carbohydrates 3.0g; Dietary fiber 0.8g; Total fat 2.3g; Saturated fat 0.8g; Cholesterol 2.4mg; Sodium 35.2mg.

Vegetarian Broth

Vegetables, mushrooms, or roasted vegetables, are the basis of these broths. They're not only tasty, but they're economical and low in fat, and extremely versatile. You can use them in almost any soup.

Vegetable Broth

This super, straightforward vegetarian broth is for general use. You can add or substitute other vegetables that you like. The recipe can be doubled.

Yield: *About 2 quarts*

Level: *Easy*

Cooking time: *1½ to 2 hours*

Freezes well for 4 to 6 months

1 large potato, cut into chunks

2 medium carrots, cut into chunks

1 to 2 small parsnips, cut into chunks

2 celery stalks with leaves attached, cut into chunks

2 medium leeks, washed and cut into chunks

1 medium onion, sliced

1⅓ cups mushroom stems, but not shiitake (optional)

3 sprigs parsley

1 bay leaf

1 teaspoon black peppercorns

2½ to 3 quarts water

1 In a large stockpot, combine the potato, carrots, parsnips, celery, leeks, onion, mushroom stems, parsley, bay leaf, and peppercorns. Add the water to cover.

2 Over medium-high heat, bring to a boil. When the liquid boils, reduce the heat to medium-low, and simmer for 50 to 60 minutes.

3 Strain the broth and press gently on the vegetables in the sieve with the back of a wooden spoon. Discard the solid ingredients. Use the broth immediately or cool, uncovered, by placing the pot in an ice bath and stirring the broth. Refrigerate the broth and use within 3 days or freeze.

Tip: *When making a vegetable broth for general use, do not include cauliflower, broccoli, cabbage, turnips, or beets because they will discolor the broth and/or impart too strong a taste.*

Per Serving: Calories 30.7; Protein 0.7g; Carbohydrates 7.2g; Dietary fiber 1.0g; Total fat 0.1g; Saturated fat 0.0g; Cholesterol 0mg; Sodium 20.7mg.

Mushroom Broth

This full-bodied broth is a natural in mushroom and vegetable soups and for vegetarian versions of legume soups such as split pea or lentil. Although you can use whole mushrooms, using mushrooms stems is more economical, and you can reserve the caps for other dishes. However, please don't use stems from shiitakes as they can impart an unpleasant flavor to the broth.

Yield: *1 to 1½ quarts*

Level: *Easy*

Cooking time: *30 to 40 minutes*

Freezes well up to 4 months

6 cups water (or canned low-sodium chicken broth)

1 cup chopped fresh mushroom stems (not shiitake stems) or mushrooms

6 to 8 dried mushrooms, such as porcini or shiitake

1 celery stalk, coarsely chopped

1 small carrot, coarsely chopped

1 small onion, peeled and thinly sliced

1 In a medium saucepan over medium heat, combine the water, mushroom stems, dried mushrooms, celery, carrot, and onion. Bring to a boil and reduce the heat to medium-low so that the liquid barely bubbles. Simmer for 20 to 30 minutes.

2 Strain the broth and discard the solids. Use the broth immediately or cool, uncovered, by placing the pot in an ice bath and stirring the broth. Refrigerate the broth and use within 3 days or freeze.

Tip: *With a hearty, almost meaty flavor, this broth can be a replacement for beef or chicken broth in many recipes. When made with water, it is a flavorful vegetarian broth to use as an alternative to vegetable broth.*

Per Serving: *Calories 19.1; Protein 0.7g; Carbohydrates 4.6g; Dietary fiber 1.0g; Total fat 0.1g; Saturated fat 0.0g; Cholesterol 0mg; Sodium 18.7mg.*

Roasted Vegetable Broth

Yield: *About 2 quarts*

Level: *Easy*

Time: *1½ to 2 hours*

Freezes well for 4 to 6 months

1 large potato, cut into chunks

2 medium carrots, cut into chunks

1 to 2 small parsnips, cut into chunks

2 celery stalks with leaves attached, cut into chunks

2 medium leeks, washed and cut into chunks

1 medium onion, sliced

1⅓ cups mushroom stems, not shiitake (optional)

2½ to 3 quarts water

3 sprigs parsley

1 bay leaf

1 teaspoon black peppercorns

1 Roast the vegetables in a 400 degrees F oven for 25 to 45 minutes, turning the vegetables occasionally so that they don't burn.

2 After the veggies are browned, transfer them to a large soup or stock pot. Deglaze the roasting pan with water. Add the rich brown liquid to the pot.

3 Cover the vegetables with water. Add the parsley, bay leaf, and peppercorns. Over medium-high heat, bring the liquid to a boil. After the liquid comes to a boil, reduce the heat to medium-low and simmer for about 50 to 60 minutes.

4 Strain the broth and press gently on the vegetables in the sieve with the back of a wooden spoon. Discard the solid ingredients. Use the broth immediately or cool by placing the pot, uncovered, in an ice bath and stirring the broth. Refrigerate the broth and use within 3 days or freeze.

Per Serving: *Calories 69.9; Protein 1.6g; Carbohydrates 16.3g; Dietary fiber 2.9g; Total fat 0.2g; Saturated fat 0.0g; Cholesterol 0mg; Sodium 85.7mg.*

Fish and Shellfish Broth

Seafood broth is highly flavored yet light and surprisingly quick and easy to make. The only trick is to make sure the broth doesn't boil.

Fish Broth

This broth is one of the fastest to make. Ask the fishmonger at the market for bones. If you are making a recipe that calls for shrimp, save the shells and use them in the broth (or store them in the freezer until you're ready to make this broth). This recipe can be doubled.

Yield: *About 1½ quarts*

Level: *Easy to intermediate*

Cooking time: *30 to 45 minutes*

Freezes well for 2 months

1½ pounds fish bones, from mild-flavored fish such as sea bass, cod, grouper, monkfish, sole, snapper, and scrod

1 celery stalk with leaves attached, cut into chunks

1 small onion, peeled and halved

1 leek, washed and cut into chunks

1 bay leaf

1 to 2 cups shrimp shells (optional)

5 to 6 cups water

1 cup dry white wine, vermouth, or additional water

1 In a medium stockpot or Dutch oven, combine the bones, celery, onion, leek, bay leaf, shrimp shells (if using), water, and wine to cover.

2 Over medium-high heat, bring to a gentle boil and immediately reduce the heat to medium-low so that the liquid barely bubbles. Simmer for 20 to 30 minutes.

3 Strain the broth and discard the solid ingredients. Use the broth immediately or cool, uncovered, by placing the pot in an ice bath and stirring the broth. Refrigerate it and use within 2 days or freeze.

Warning: *Never boil fish broth or it will become so cloudy and take on an unappealing taste that it would ruin your soup. If this happens, you'll have to start again from scratch.*

Per Serving: *Calories 14.4; Protein 0.4g; Carbohydrates 3.1g; Dietary fiber 0.5g; Total fat 0.1g; Saturated fat 0.0g; Cholesterol 0mg; Sodium 17.3mg; Notes: Wine reflects alcohol evaporation; analysis is per cup.*

Shrimp Broth

Full of shrimp flavor, this simple broth is not only quick but also very easy to prepare. It's a fine substitute for fish broth in the soup recipes in this book.

Yield: *1 to 1½ quarts*

Level: *Easy*

Cooking time: *30 minutes*

Do not freeze

6 cups canned low-sodium chicken broth

shells from ½ to 1 pound of shrimp

1 celery stalk, coarsely chopped

1 small carrot, coarsely chopped

1 small onion, peeled and halved

1 In a large saucepan over medium heat, combine the broth, shrimp shells, celery, carrot, and onion. Bring to a gentle boil and immediately reduce the heat to medium-low so that the liquid barely bubbles. Simmer for 20 to 30 minutes.

2 Strain the broth and discard the solids. Use the broth immediately or cool, uncovered, by placing the pot in an ice bath and stirring the broth. Refrigerate it and use within 2 days or freeze.

Per Serving: *Calories 37.1; Protein 3.3g; Carbohydrates 3.0g; Dietary fiber 0.4g; Total fat 1.5g; Saturated fat 0.8g; Cholesterol 3.8mg; Sodium 115.4mg.*

Clam Broth

Use this broth in recipes for clam chowders or as an alternative to fish broth when you're in a hurry.

Yield: *Any amount*

Level: *Easy*

Preparation time: *5 minutes*

Do not freeze

bottled clam juice   water

1 Combine equal amounts of clam juice and water to make the amount you need for a recipe. For example, you may use 1 cup clam juice and 1 cup water.

Per Serving: *Calories 0g; Protein 0g; Carbohydrates 0g; Dietary fiber 0g; Total fat 0g; Saturated fat 0g; Cholesterol 0mg; Sodium 563.6mg.*

Basic Dashi

Dashi is the broth used in most Japanese soups and will impart an authentic taste. The ingredients for making it can be found in Asian or Japanese grocery stores. You can also purchase instant dashi that can be added to boiling water.

Yield: 4 to 4½ cups

Level: Easy to intermediate

Preparation time: 10 minutes

Do not freeze

3 to 4 inch piece dried kelp or kombu

4 to 4½ cups cold water

½ to 1 cup dried bonito fish flakes

1 Wipe the dried kelp with a damp cloth, taking care not to remove its white powdery coating. With scissors, cut the kelp into several strips.

2 In a medium pot over medium heat, combine 4 cups of water and the dried kelp. When the water starts to boil, remove the dried kelp with tongs or a slotted spoon, and discard it.

3 Add the remaining ½ cup cold water and the bonita flakes. When the water returns to a boil, immediately remove the pot from the heat and set it aside.

4 After the bonita flakes have sunk to the bottom of the pot, about 3 minutes, strain the dashi through a strainer lined with cheesecloth or a fine mesh sieve. Discard the solids and use the broth immediately.

Warning: Do not boil the dashi. Don't cover the pot to return the water to a boil faster, or the dashi will have an unpleasant taste and become cloudy. If this happens, you must toss out the dashi and start again from scratch.

Per Serving: Calories 32.9; Protein 3.4g; Carbohydrates 1.6g; Dietary fiber 0.2g; Total fat 1.4g; Saturated fat 0.2g; Cholesterol 7.7mg; Sodium 465.9mg.

Chapter 6

Soup Safety

. . . .

In This Chapter

▶ Chilling broth and soup safely

▶ Storing and freezing broth and soup

▶ Thawing and reheating safely

. . . .

*F*ood follows the golden rule: How you treat it is how it'll end up treating you. You may not want to use or eat a soup or broth immediately after cooking it. Perhaps you want to keep it for later in the week or freeze it. But don't just let it sit on the back of the stove. It's very important to handle food properly to prevent bacterial growth, and broth is no exception. Don't fret — you can take a few easy steps to prevent any potential contamination.

✔ Broth, as well as meat, poultry, vegetable, and creamy soups, can be refrigerated for up to three days.

✔ Vegetable purees and legume soups can be refrigerated for up to four days.

Chilling Safely

When you're not going to use broth or soup right away, it's essential to chill it down properly. Putting any food, especially hot broth or soup, directly into the refrigerator or freezer is unwise. The residual heat can raise the temperature inside the fridge, and not only the soup, but also other items can spoil. It's important to chill soup or broth quickly and refrigerate or freeze it as soon as it's cooled. Left at room temperature for too long, food becomes a breeding ground for bacteria. These easy steps can help you keep food safe and tasting its best.

✔ To cool broth or soup, fill a kitchen sink one-third full with very cold water. Add a few trays of ice cubes to the water to make it frigid. Put the pot directly into this ice-water bath, but be careful that the water doesn't spill over into the pot. This step is essential for broth or soup that you're not using right away. If you're only storing it for a future meal, ice it down! An ice-water bath makes broth, soup, and stew cool down much faster for storage.

✔ Use a ladle or spoon to stir the broth or soup until it cools down to lukewarm — cool enough that you can poke your clean finger in it and it doesn't feel hot. When you stir the soup, bring the liquid from the bottom to the top, so the temperature reduces evenly and more quickly.

✔ Transfer the cooled broth or soup to another container that it fills almost completely (about ½ to 1 inch to spare) and cover it.

✔ If you've made soup in a stainless or enamel coated pot, you can put the covered pot in the fridge for a few hours or overnight after it's cooled, and then transfer it to a more suitable container the next morning.

✔ Promptly refrigerate or freeze cooled broth or soup.

Storage Containers

What's the best vessel in which to store broth or soup? Here's a breakdown:

✔ For refrigerator storage, use a stainless steel, plastic, porcelain, or glass container, covered with a tight-fitting lid or plastic wrap.

✔ For freezer storage, use self-sealing freezer bags or freezer-proof plastic containers with lids that have a tight seal.

✔ Don't store broth or soup in aluminum or cast iron because these materials will impart an unpleasant or metallic taste to the food.

Some people like to freeze broth in ice cube trays and keep the resulting broth cubes in a self-sealing plastic bag. You can combine a few cubes for a warming cup of broth. They're also great for recipes where you need only a small amount, such as sauce recipes.

Keep the fat

Excess fat will solidify on the surface after the broth or soup is cold. The fat actually seals and protects it from bacteria. Leave the fat until you're ready to use the broth, then remove and discard it before heating. If you're planning to freeze the soup or broth, leave the fat on top as an extra guard against freezer burn and remove it after thawing.

Freezing Basics

Freezing is the most convenient way to store leftovers for future meals. These practical tips can help you do it correctly:

- ✔ When the broth or soup is cooled, you can transfer it to freezer-proof containers.

- ✔ Use containers that are the right size — individual portions for quick meals and pint-size or quart-size containers for larger batches.

- ✔ Food expands when it freezes. Ideally, broth or soup should nearly fill its container. Ladle soup into the container so that a gap of ½ to 1 inch remains at the top.

- ✔ Close the container, open it partially to release any trapped or excess air, and then seal it well. If using self-sealing bags, fill the bag about halfway to two thirds full, release as much air as you can, and then seal.

If the lid has popped off a container in the freezer, you probably overfilled the container. In most cases, freezer burn has developed. The surface will look cracked and possibly parched. Often, many ice crystals have formed on top. Food with freezer burn tastes odd and should be discarded.

Table 6-1 shows how long broth and soup can be frozen.

Table 6-1	Freezing Times for Soups and Broths
Type of Soup	*Freezing Time*
Broth	Up to 6 months
Pureed vegetable soups	Up to 3 months
Legume soups	Up to 2 months
Creamy soups	Up to 2 months
Brothy, multi-ingredient soups	1 to 2 months
Seafood soups	Best eaten fresh or within 3 days

Thawing

You can thaw soup in several different ways. They all work equally well, but some are faster.

- Thaw overnight in the refrigerator.
- Thaw in the microwave, following the directions for your unit.
- Thaw uncovered on the counter until softened and mostly liquid, and then reheat or finish thawing in the refrigerator.

Don't let already thawed food stand at room temperature for hours or bacteria may begin to form. Refrigerate it until you're ready to reheat or cook it.

Simple Suggestions for Reheating

You can reheat soups and broths in a number of ways, including these:

- Reheat broth and soup over medium heat, stirring occasionally.
- Bring broth and soup up to a boil to kill any bacteria that may have accumulated if it has been stored improperly, and then reduce the heat and simmer.
- If any ingredients start to stick to the pot, stir and reduce the heat to medium-low.
- When reheating, add extra liquid if you see the soup's become too thick.

Chapter 7

Playing with Your Food

*B*e honest. Who doesn't like to play with food? Whether out of a sense of adventure (How would curry taste?) or from sheer necessity (the store was out of green beans), making up a dish is the uncharted territory we all enter at one time or another. When it comes to soup, this is certainly not a new or radical process, but actually it's a well-established tradition through-out Europe, particularly in parts of France and Switzerland. There, in home and restaurant kitchens alike, the soup pot is always simmering on the stove, and cooks add ingredients daily, some fresh, some leftovers, altering the com-binations to create a new soup du jour every day!

Improvising and substituting ingredients can be both a daunting and rewarding event, but by all means, let it be fun. Your experience is certainly helpful, and common sense is your biggest ally when embarking on this culinary journey into the unknown. Perhaps you won't want to try it when company's coming, but maybe that depends on who's coming. I can offer a few hints that will get you started and point you in the right direction, but after that, you're on your own. With a little practice, you will be able to make your own concoctions.

Perhaps you want to try to imitate something you've eaten in a restaurant or perhaps you just want to let your own imagination go wild. Browse through a few recipes, check your kitchen inventory, and get going.

My only advice is this: Keep it simple. The flavors should be pure, clean, and fresh tasting. This is not the time to try to become an expert on ethnic or cross-cultural cuisine by combining spices and herbs that you're unsure of or to blend Asian ingredients with Italian. When the soup is finished and you like it, and your friends rave about your culinary talents, your worry lines will vanish. You may even consider doing it again.

Halving and Doubling Recipes

Changing the quantity that you make may be one of your first improvisations. Suppose that you would like to make some lentil or bean soup, but you don't want to make a full batch because you want it today only and your freezer compartment is already overloaded. Or perhaps you're having a crowd and want to make a double batch. Here's the hitch: Recipes don't always scale up or down in perfect proportion. You need to make a few minor adjustments.

Halving

When halving a recipe, be aware that you might need to alter the seasonings as well as the amount of liquid. Start with half of the specified quantity, and add a little more if necessary. The cooking time might also be a little less than if you were making a full recipe, so pay closer attention while simmering. If the recipe starts with sautéed onions, you might need a bit more than half of the vegetable oil or butter.

When halving or doubling a recipe, sometimes you'll end up with unused raw veggies. If the ingredient list states 1 medium onion, chopped or 1 medium carrot, chopped, why keep half an onion or carrot in the fridge when you can use a small one instead? Conversely, if double the amount requires 4 celery stalks and 2 cups of green beans, but you only have 3 celery stalks and 2¼ cups of green beans, use what you have and keep going.

Doubling

When doubling a recipe, make sure that you have a pot that's large enough or divide the mixture evenly into two pots. You'll probably then need to adjust the cooking time. If you use a very large pot, know that the cooking time will definitely increase, because it will take longer for the liquid to come to a boil.

If you're making the soup in one large pot you won't need to double the amount of vegetable oil or butter, but only use slightly more. You'll also need to check the amount of liquid while it's cooking to see whether you need to add some more or perhaps take out a ladleful, keeping what you removed handy in the event that you need to return it to the pot.

Don't just double the seasonings; taste the soup as it cooks. Ingredients such as bay leaves don't necessarily need to be doubled at all. You can get by with 1 or 1½ at most. If the soup has fresh chilies, you might want to try it with 1½ times the amount. The same goes for cayenne pepper or chili powder.

Salt and pepper are the biggest challenges. I don't give you an exact scale up here. Remember to add them in small increments, and taste, taste, taste. Changing the quantity is not really that difficult, but it does require a little extra attention. You'll soon get the hang of it.

When halving or doubling a recipe, write the ingredient list on a piece of paper with the quantities that you will be using. It's too easy to make a mistake if you simply do it in your head as you go along.

Making Pureed Soups

Pureed vegetable soups are a snap to make and allow you to take advantage of whatever is in your fridge. Think about what might taste good together or what ingredients you've combined in recipes that you've already mastered. Look at what you have on hand, and set your mind free to come up with some suggestions. You might make a flop, but you might make a winner!

Making the most of what you have

If you have some fresh vegetables that you'd like to turn into a pureed soup, sauté an onion, carrot, and celery stalk, add a bit of white wine (or not), and some broth. Bring to a boil, and add the vegetables and herbs or spices. Reduce the heat, and simmer until the veggies are tender. Puree with a hand blender or in batches in a food processor or blender. Thicken soups if necessary by adding mashed potatoes or adding up to ½ cup cooked rice to the soup before pureeing. Add cream, sour cream, or yogurt, and season with salt and pepper.

Leftover remakes

Have a little fun. Maybe you have bowls of leftover veggies that are great material for your concoction — some cooked potatoes, cauliflower, carrots, and green beans. Maybe you have some rice left over from Chinese takeout and half a head of lettuce, or yesterday's zucchini and scallion stir-fry with a hint of ginger. These are the basic ingredients for two potential soups, both different. You can simmer each set of ingredients in some chicken or vegetable broth, add a few herbs such as thyme, parsley, or chives to the first set, and puree each with a hand blender or in a food processor. Add a little milk or cream to the first soup and maybe a hint of sherry or soy sauce to the second. Taste for seasoning. You've got two homemade soups, and almost as fast as opening a can.

Leftovers are usually already seasoned with salt, pepper, and other herbs or spices. Keep this in mind when you combine them in soup so that you don't mix conflicting flavors. Taste and use a light hand when seasoning the soup.

Everything but the Kitchen Sink

Sometimes you don't feel like following a recipe. You want to make soup, and you can make a simple soup. Your best bet is to skim through several recipes before you begin. Get some ideas and inspiration.

Try this suggestion: Start with the aromatic vegetable combination (chopped onion, carrot, and celery or one of its variations with bell pepper or scallions or leeks), and sauté the veggies in a tablespoon or two of olive or vegetable oil. Add a clove or two of minced garlic. Add the broth, vegetables, meat or leftover cooked poultry, and some noodles or rice. Bring to a boil, reduce the heat so that the soup simmers, and cover partially. Simmer until everything is cooked.

If you want to use items that cook quickly, such as shrimp, fish, snow peas, and the like, make sure that you add them toward the end of the cooking time. These items take only a few minutes to cook or reheat.

You've got great timing

Timing isn't everything, but it sure helps when you're improvising so that you don't end up with uncooked food or mush. When putting ingredients together, think of how long each item takes to cook individually and then add them to your soup in the correct order.

Table 7-1 shows the average timing for some common ingredients.

Table 7-1	Cooking Times for Common Foods
Ingredient	*Cooking Time*
Rice, white	15 to 20 minutes
Rice, brown and wild	45 to 55 minutes
Pearl barley	45 to 55 minutes
Pasta and noodles, dried	8 to 12 minutes
Pasta and noodles, fresh	2 to 8 minutes
Potatoes, white and sweet, cubed	15 to 30 minutes, depending on size

Ingredient	Cooking Time
Dried lentils	15 to 45 minutes, depending on type
Dried beans and split peas	1½ to 2 hours (plus soaking time)
Root vegetables, cubed	15 to 35 minutes, depending on size
Beets	35 minutes to 1 hour, depending on size
Cabbage	40 minutes to 1 hour
Broccoli and cauliflower	10 minutes for just-tender and crunchy, up to 45 minutes if for puree
Butternut squash, peeled and cubed	20 to 25 minutes
Spinach, snow peas, and sugar snap peas	2 to 5 minutes
Zucchini, yellow squash, and green beans	5 to 12 minutes, depending on size
Carrots and celery	up to 25 to 30 minutes
Tomatoes	up to 30 to 35 minutes for fresh
Chicken parts	30 to 50 minutes
Chicken, boneless	15 to 25 minutes
Cooked chicken	10 to 15 minutes
Beef or lamb cubes	1½ to 2 hours
Shrimp	5 minutes
Fish	10 to 15 minutes

Substituting ingredients

What do you do when you dislike a particular ingredient in a recipe or you're out of an item? Substitute it, of course, with something that you enjoy eating. Try to use an ingredient that has a similar texture and cooking time. Table 7-2 has some ideas.

Table 7-2	Substitutions Allowed!
Ingredient	Substitution
Chicken breasts, boneless and skinless	Chicken thighs, boneless and skinless
Chicken, cooked, shredded, or cubed	Turkey, cooked, shredded, or cubed

(continued)

Table 7-2 (continued)

Ingredient	Substitution
Beef bottom round, cubed	Beef chuck, cubed
White fish, firm	Cod, scrod, halibut, haddock, catfish
White fish, soft	Flounder, sea bass, sole, trout
Butternut squash	Acorn squash
Cauliflower or broccoli	Broccoflower, Savoy cabbage, Green cabbage
Snow peas	Sugar snap peas
Green beans	Wax beans
Zucchini	Yellow squash
Sweet potatoes	Yams, butternut squash, or potatoes
White potatoes	Baby potatoes or sweet potatoes
Turnips	Rutabaga or parsnips
Spinach	Swiss chard, sorrel, or watercress
Bell peppers	Use colors interchangeably
Romaine lettuce	Escarole
Small pasta shells	Small macaroni or ditalini
Thin egg noodles	Angel hair, fidelos, or ramen
Rice, white	Basmati rice
Tomatoes, peeled, seeded, and chopped	Canned tomatoes, chopped or whole, broken up with a spoon
Tomatoes, pureed	Tomato sauce
Fresh corn, green beans, peas, or lima beans	Frozen vegetables
Dry beans, cooked	Canned beans, drained and rinsed
Dry white wine	Dry white vermouth
Salt	Salt substitute
Eggs	Egg substitute
Cream	Half-and-Half, milk, 2% milk
Sour Cream	Nonfat sour cream or yogurt
Apple juice	Apple cider or white grape juice

If a recipe calls for wine or sherry, never substitute cooking wine or cooking sherry. Neither add a true wine taste, and they contain a large amount of sodium. A good rule for cooking with alcohol is not to cook with any wine that you wouldn't also drink.

Make It Vegetarian

Sometimes, you want to make a soup vegetarian. Maybe a friend is coming over who doesn't eat meat. I often turn legume soups into vegetarian meals. Omit the ham hock or sausage, and follow the instructions. (You'll find legume soup recipes in Chapter 8.) You might want to add an extra clove of garlic, half a seeded, minced jalapeno, or a pinch more herbs in the beginning, or a little extra salt or pepper to the soup after it's cooked.

It's simply not possible to convert hearty meat soups or fish soups. However, I've had wonderful success with many soups that don't contain meat, such as cream soups, vegetable purees, or vegetable soups that utilize chicken broth. These can easily become vegetarian delights. Replace the chicken broth with vegetable broth, mushroom broth, or roasted vegetable broth. In some of the Asian soup recipes in this book, I've already made suggestions to omit cooked, shredded chicken and replace it with tofu.

Lighten Up with Less Fat

The recipes in the book use only the fat that's necessary for cooking and that will still let the finished soup taste best. Due to dietary concerns, some people may still want or need to lighten up further. Use these general tips:

- ✔ Cook in nonstick pans. You can use slightly less vegetable or olive oil or butter than is called for.

- ✔ Trim meat and poultry of all visible fat.

- ✔ Replace cream, half-and-half, or whole milk products with low-fat, skim, or nonfat dairy products. Note that low-fat cheeses don't melt as smoothly, so they might not be a wise choice.

- ✔ Chill soup and broth and remove any visible fat from the surface. Reheat before serving. Chill canned broth as well, and remove any fat, minimal though it may be, before using.

Part III
Alphabet Soup

The 5th Wave   By Rich Tennant

"OK Cookie-your venison in lingdonberry sauce is good, as are your eggplant souffle and the risotto with foie gras. But whoever taught you how to make a croquembouche should be shot!"

In this part . . .

The chapters in this section will give you intimate knowledge of ordinary and exotic food from the garden to the spice shelf and everything in between. Do you know what to look for in a tomato? How about in a chicken? And what's the best way to keep herbs fresh? If you want to make good soup, you've got to get on more than speaking terms with things you formerly passed by or took for granted — you need to know them in depth.

Chapter 8

Homemade Soup off the Shelf

All the ingredients highlighted in this chapter have a long shelf-life, which means that you can buy them in bulk and not worry about them going bad quickly. Most should be kept in sealed containers in a cool, dry place, such as a kitchen cupboard or cabinet.

Canned goods, such as tomatoes, fish, and broth, are the most commonly stored items. All cans should be without dents because dents sometimes conceal small holes, invisible to the eye, through which airborne bacteria can enter and cause the food inside to spoil. Sometimes, labels have use-by dates, so check for them.

You'll find an abundance of other shelf-stable items that aren't processed or canned that are perfect for soup. These include dried foods and staples such as vegetable oils, rice, pastas, grains as well as legumes.

Olive and Other Vegetable Oils

Olive oil is considered one of the most healthful of all oils. A staple of Mediterranean cuisine, it is a must for any kitchen. Wonderful in cooking and in dressings, its color can range from deep green to pale gold. The less refined the oil — such as the extra virgin olive oil yielded by the first pressing — then the stronger the flavor and the higher the cost. Many grades of olive oil are on the market, and you need to be aware of what you're buying and how it's best used. Sometimes, another vegetable oil is a better choice. Peanut and olive oil have high "burn points," which means that either is a good choice for sautéing. Other frequently used oils include corn, safflower, and canola. Store them in a cool cupboard.

Breakdown of commonly-used cooking oils

These oils are commonly used in cooking. You may want to have several of these on hand for different uses.

Extra virgin olive oil comes from the first pressing and tends to have a strong, fruity aroma and taste. It should be reserved for salad dressings, pesto, and as a condiment for drizzling on fish, pasta, vegetables, and chicken.

Virgin olive oil comes from the second pressing and has a milder but still a rich, full-bodied taste. It is perfect for sautéing most items.

Pure olive oil is more refined, and although it's not as flavorful, it can still be used for sautéing.

Extra-light olive oil is heavily processed and extremely mild and pale. Don't be fooled — it doesn't have fewer calories than other oils, just less taste. Use another, cheaper vegetable oil instead.

Vegetable oils, such as canola, safflower, corn, and peanut, range in color from yellow to gold and are flavorless. They are excellent all-purpose oils for general cooking and are less expensive than olive oil. They can be used interchangeably, but it's worth noting that canola oil has the highest level of monounsaturated fat.

If you live where it's very hot and humid, you might want to keep cooking oils in the refrigerator in summer. They can become rancid. Always store oils that you don't often use, especially strong-flavored oils such as Chinese toasted sesame oil, in the fridge.

Olive oil is a monounsaturated fat, believed to help reduce the LDL cholesterol levels in your blood. Canola is the next highest oil in terms of monounsaturated fats, and peanut oil is about half monounsaturated. Polyunsaturated fats include corn, soy, safflower, and sesame oils. Although healthier than hydrogenated fats, such as margarine, or saturated fats such as butter, they possess no cholesterol-lowering properties.

Rather than buying aerosol vegetable oil sprays for cooking and baking, try filling a kitchen oil sprayer (available at many cookware shops) with olive or vegetable oil.

Rice

Rice is one of the world's most popular dietary staples and is a welcome addition to soup. It too has a long shelf life when stored correctly. If you plan to use rice often, you can keep it in its box; otherwise, transfer it to a container after it is opened.

Rice is porous and absorbs other flavors with which it comes in contact. Make sure that you don't store it near your spices or it may end up tasting like curry powder or cinnamon. But this trait has benefits too and can transform ordinary rice into a luxury item. Flavor your rice by storing it with a few dried wild mushrooms, such as morels or porcinis, or if you're extravagant, truffles — ooh la la. This is particularly good for arborio rice that's for risotto. You can use the truffles or mushrooms in another dish after you've used all the rice. Store flavored rice in a sealed glass or plastic container and label it.

The raw or the cooked?

Although this might seem obvious, I've been asked this question several times. When uncooked or raw rice is called for, the recipe will simply call for X amount of *rice,* but when cooked rice is required, it will specify X amount of *cooked rice.*

Several types of rice are suitable for soup. Let the following sections point you in the right direction.

White rice

White rice is polished, which means the germ and bran have been removed. Two types of white rice are available: long-grain, with grains that remain separate after cooking, and short-grain, with grains that stick together after cooking. Use all-purpose, long-grain white rice for most soups where white rice is specified. For a nuttier taste, try basmati or Texmati. Jasmine, the sweet-tasting Thai rice, and arborio, the popular short-grain white rice used in risotto, are not appropriate for the soup recipes in this book. White rice takes about 15 to 20 minutes to cook.

Brown rice

Brown rice is unmilled or unpolished rice and is slightly more nutritious than white rice because the germ and bran are intact. It has a richer taste and firmer texture and takes about 45 to 55 minutes to cook. Quick brown rice, which takes about 15 to 20 minutes to cook, is also available in many markets, and this type can be substituted for white rice in soup because their cooking times are similar. In recipes where cooked rice is called for, you may substitute cooked brown rice.

Wild rice

Early settlers believed that wild rice, the seed of a long-grain marsh grass, native to the northern Great Lakes region, resembled rice and accordingly named it wild rice. It has a unique, nutty taste that is wonderful with mushrooms. Traditionally harvested by Native Americans, it is also being produced commercially. It can be expensive, so if it's beyond your budget, use equal parts of wild and brown or white rice. The cooking time is 50 to 60 minutes, and wild rice shouldn't be used in soup unless specified.

Barley

Cultivated and eaten since the Stone Age, this delicious and filling grain is rich in both protein and B vitamins. Although not specifically a rice, barley fulfills a similar function in soup. Pearl (or pearled) barley is the type most readily available. Although its bran has been removed for easier and shorter cooking, it still has good nutritional value. Stored in an airtight container, pearled barley should last for 9 to 12 months, sometimes longer.

Pasta

In soup, you'll probably use dried pastas or noodles instead of freshly made. Stored in a cool, dry place, dried pasta will keep almost indefinitely. Noodles or pasta rarely need to be prepared separately, but are added directly to the soup and cooked. Small-shapes or miniature pasta, as opposed to long noodles, are most often called for in soups. Use small shells, small elbow macaroni, ditalini (small tubes), thin egg noodles, wide egg noodles, or tortellini as specified.

Naturally, there's an exception to this rule — Asian noodle soups require long, ramen-style noodles. If the noodles are too long for you to eat comfortably, you can break them before cooking. Other Asian noodles sometimes used in soup are rice noodles or rice sticks. These have a short cooking time, and you must adjust timing in recipes accordingly if you substitute them in any of the Asian soup recipes in the book. Mung bean noodles, also called bean threads, must be soaked in a bowl of hot water for about 20 minutes and drained. Then you add them directly to fully cooked soup right before serving.

Legumes: Beans, Lentils, and Split Peas

Legumes are not vegetables; they are actually pod-ripened seeds with more culinary virtues than many other foods. Many varieties exist (see Figure 8-1), but the most well known are beans, lentils, peas, and peanuts. With high nutritional value, legumes are a dietary staple throughout the world. Some varieties, such as soybeans, are high in protein, and most are high in fiber and carbohydrates. Legumes are a remarkably rich source of B vitamins and minerals such as iron and calcium.

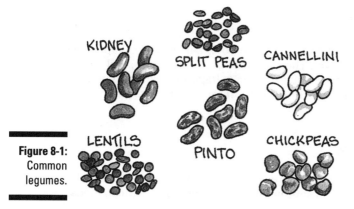

Figure 8-1:
Common
legumes.

Always marvelous in soup, inexpensive, and nutritious, legumes can be pur-chased in 1- or 2-pound bags at the supermarket or loose in many health food and ethnic grocery stores. If you buy them in bags, store them that way. But if you buy in bulk, keep legumes in sealed glass or plastic containers. Either way, they will last in your cabinet for a year or more. The varieties of beans are numerous, but here's a compendium of those called for in the recipes in this chapter.

Black beans

Widely used in Latin American, Mexican, and Caribbean cuisine, black beans are kidney shaped and actually have a white flesh. Their rich and earthy taste can stand up to hot chilies, spices, and garlic.

Legume equivalents

At some point, you'll probably want to know how many beans you'll end up with when you cook dried ones or how many cups are really in a can. Here's a handy guide:

- 1 pound dried beans = 2–2½ cups uncooked and becomes 6½–7½ cups when cooked

- 1 pound dried lentils or split peas = 2½ cups uncooked and becomes 7–7½ cups when cooked

- One 15–16-ounce can, rinsed and drained = 1½–1¾ cups cooked beans

- One 20-ounce can, rinsed and drained = 2 cups

Chickpeas

Also known as Garbanzo beans, these round, irregularly shaped beans have a mild, nutty flavor. They are used in soups, salads, and stews of Mediterranean countries, such as Spain, Italy, Morocco, and in the Middle East, as well as in recipes from Latin America and India.

Pinto beans

These kidney-shaped beans are beige or pink and dotted with dark brown flecks. They are used in southwestern, Tex-Mex, and Mexican foods.

Red kidney beans, small red beans, and pink beans

These meaty beans can be used interchangeably and may be substituted where pinto beans are listed as an ingredient. Although not traditional, they can replace white beans in minestrone.

White beans

You can find many kinds of white beans, all having a mild flavor and somewhat creamy texture. Use great northern, navy, or white kidney beans interchangeably. (White kidney beans are also called by their Italian name, cannellini.)

Brown lentils

These common lentils are sold everywhere and are suitable for the soup recipes in this book. The smaller French green lentils and red lentils are not a substitute.

Split peas

Green peas have an intense pea taste, but their yellow cousins are somewhat milder. Both are most often found split, although you can find them whole in some markets.

Sorting beans

Pebbles are often hidden amongst the beans. To prevent a cracked tooth, you must sort through them. Put the beans in a colander and rinse under cold running water. Pick through to remove any pebbles or debris, as well as any discolored and shriveled beans.

Soaking

To soak or not to soak, that is the question. No matter what the color — red, green, brown, or yellow — lentils and dried split peas don't need any pre-soaking and can be used after washing and picking over. However, whole dried peas do benefit from soaking. Some cookbooks and chefs refer to this process as presoaking.

I nearly always soak dried beans. Although some respected, modern chefs don't see the advantage, soaking does remove a percentage, albeit small, of the gas-producing sugars that can cause digestive problems and bloating for some people.

The overnight soaking method

Put the beans in a large pot and add water until the water level is approximately 3 inches above the beans. Soak overnight. Drain and cover again with fresh water to cook.

The quick soaking method

Put the beans in a large pot and add water until the water level is approximately 2–3 inches above the beans. Over high heat, bring to a boil and cook for 2 minutes. Remove the pot from the heat and let the beans stand in the water for 1 hour before using. Drain and cover again with fresh water to cook.

When cooking fresh legumes, adding salt or acidic foods, such as tomatoes, vinegar, or wine, can make them toughen and take much longer to cook. Add these ingredients to the pot after the beans are already tender. Simmer a while longer until their flavors are fully incorporated.

Canned beans

Although their texture is somewhat softer than freshly cooked dried beans, canned beans are timesaving, convenient, and still make a good soup. Before using, put the canned beans in a sieve or colander and pour off the canning liquid. Rinse them well under cold, running water and drain.

Legume Soups

Legumes can easily be transformed into marvelous, filling soups that generally freeze well. Sometimes, legume soups get too thick during cooking or after storing, but a little extra water or broth restores them to the right consistency.

Yellow Pea Soup

A hint of garlic, thyme, and mustard pep up this warming soup. For a vegetarian version, omit the ham hock.

Serves: *6 to 8*

Level: *Easy*

Special equipment: *Food processor, blender, or hand blender*

Preparation time: *30 minutes*

Cooking time: *1½ to 2 hours*

Freezes well

1 pound dried yellow split peas, rinsed and picked over	3 tablespoons minced fresh parsley
8 cups water	1½ teaspoons minced fresh thyme or ¾ teaspoon dried thyme
1 small ham hock (optional)	1¼ teaspoons Dijon mustard
2 medium onions, chopped	Salt to taste, about ½–1 teaspoon
1 large carrot, peeled and chopped	½ teaspoon freshly ground black pepper or to taste
2 plump cloves garlic, minced	

1 In a large pot over medium heat, combine the yellow split peas, water, and ham hock. Cover and bring to a boil. Simmer, uncovered, for 15 minutes. Skim off any foam that forms. Reduce the heat to medium-low.

2 Add the onions, carrot, garlic, parsley, thyme, and mustard. Simmer, partially covered, until the peas and ham are very tender, about 1 to 1½ hours.

3 Remove the ham and chop the meat, discarding the bone. Set the meat aside.

4 Puree the soup in batches in a food processor or blender. Alternatively, if you have a hand blender, leave the soup in the pot and blend.

5 Season with salt and pepper to taste. Return the ham to the soup if desired and reheat.

Cook's Fact: *Yellow Split Pea Soup hails from both Canada and Scandinavia, whereas green split pea soup is a Dutch treat.*

Per Serving: Calories 223.1; Protein 15.6g; Carbohydrates 41.1g; Dietary fiber 0.7g; Total fat 0.1g; Saturated fat 0.0g; Cholesterol 0mg; Sodium 178.8mg.

Old-Fashioned Split Pea Soup

This traditional winter soup should be as thick as a heavy fog. Some people don't like to puree the soup, but simply simmer it a bit longer until it has cooked down to the right consistency.

Serves: *6 to 8*

Level: *Easy*

Special equipment: *Food processor, blender, or hand blender*

Preparation time: *30 minutes*

Cooking time: *1½ to 2 hours*

Freezes well

1 pound dried split green peas, rinsed and picked over

8 cups water

1 small ham hock (optional)

2 medium onions, chopped

2 medium carrots, peeled and chopped

1 large celery stalk, chopped

1–2 plump cloves garlic, minced

¼ cup chopped parsley

1½ teaspoons minced fresh thyme or ½ teaspoon dried thyme

1 bay leaf

Salt to taste, about ½–1 teaspoon

¾ teaspoon freshly ground black pepper or to taste

Croutons for garnish, optional

1 In a large pot over medium heat, combine the green split peas, water, and ham hock. Cover and bring to a boil. Simmer, uncovered, for 15 minutes. Skim off any foam that forms. Reduce the heat to medium-low.

2 Add the onions, carrots, celery, garlic, parsley, thyme, and bay leaf. Simmer, partially covered, until the peas and ham are very tender, about 1 to 1½ hours.

3 Remove the bay leaf and discard. Remove the ham, chop the meat, and discard the bone. Set the meat aside.

4 Puree the soup in batches in a food processor or blender. Alternatively, if you have a hand blender, leave the soup in the pot and blend. Return the ham to the soup, if desired.

5 Season with salt and pepper to taste and reheat. Garnish with homemade or packaged croutons.

Cook's Fact: *Both green and yellow split peas are a type of field pea, and they are specifically grown to be dried (and turned into soup!). They are cousins of the green, common garden pea that we eat fresh.*

Per Serving: *Calories 227.6; Protein 15.8g; Carbohydrates 42.2g; Dietary fiber 1.1g; Total fat 0.1g; Saturated fat 0.0g; Cholesterol 0mg; Sodium 168.7mg.*

Spicy Peanut Soup

Peanuts, a legume known as "goobers" or "goober peas" in the deep South and ground-nuts in Africa, are the basis for this velvety soup that graced Colonial tables from Georgia to Virginia. Versions of this soup can also be found throughout West Africa. For a tasty twist, use the canned unsweetened coconut milk instead of the half-and-half.

Serves: 6

Level: Easy

Preparation time: 10 minutes

Cooking time: 25 minutes

Do not freeze

2 tablespoons vegetable oil

6 scallions, white part only, chopped; reserve chopped greens from 3 scallions for garnish

1 medium celery stalk, chopped

2 teaspoons minced fresh ginger, about ½-inch piece

1½ tablespoons all-purpose flour

4 cups chicken broth

1 cup smooth, natural peanut butter

½ cup half-and-half or unsweetened coconut milk

½–¾ teaspoon cayenne pepper

Salt to taste, about ½ teaspoon

Chopped dry roasted peanuts for garnish

1 In a large pot over medium heat, heat the vegetable oil. Add the scallions and celery and sauté, stirring occasionally, until softened, about 5 minutes. Add the ginger and cook for 2 minutes, stirring occasionally.

2 Add the flour and cook, stirring frequently, for 3 to 5 minutes.

3 Add the chicken broth and simmer until the broth is hot and slightly thickened, about 5 minutes. For a velvety texture, strain the solids and return the liquid to the pot.

4 Reduce the heat to medium-low. Add the peanut butter, half-and-half, and cayenne pepper and stir to blend. Simmer until the soup is heated through, about 5 to 7 minutes. Do not let the soup boil.

5 Season with salt to taste. Serve, garnished with peanuts and the reserved scallion greens.

Tip: Natural peanut butter contains only peanuts, oil, and sometimes salt. Although it is sold commercially, it can be easily made in a food processor by pureeing raw or roasted peanuts, preferably unsalted, with a little peanut oil until they turn into a smooth paste. If you use unsalted peanut butter in the soup, add salt to taste.

Per Serving: *Calories 354.6; Protein 12.0g; Carbohydrates 12.7g; Dietary fiber 3.3g; Total fat 30.8g; Saturated fat 5.4g; Cholesterol 10.8mg; Sodium 984.5mg.*

Vegetarian Lentil Soup

This savory lentil soup, based on an Italian recipe, has been on my winter menu for lunch or supper for many years. I like this lentil soup without meat, but you can add a small ham hock or ham bone when you add the water. Before pureeing the soup, remove the ham hock and chop and reserve its meat. Then add the chopped ham to the pureed soup before reheating. You may also garnish the vegetarian version with a drizzle of red wine vinegar, or for a nonvegetarian dish, sprinkle the vegetarian version with homemade bacon bits.

Serves: *8–10*

Level: *Easy*

Special equipment: *Food processor, blender, or hand blender*

Preparation time: *10 minutes*

Cooking time: *40 to 55 minutes*

Freezes well

2 tablespoons olive oil

2 medium carrots, peeled and chopped

2 medium celery stalks, chopped

1 medium onion, chopped

2 plump cloves garlic, minced

8 cups water

1 pound brown lentils, rinsed and picked over

One 14-ounce can chopped canned tomatoes with juice

2 tablespoons chopped fresh flat-leaf parsley

1 bay leaf

2 teaspoons minced fresh thyme or 1 teaspoon dried thyme

Salt to taste, about 1–1½ teaspoons

¾ teaspoon black pepper or to taste

Freshly ground Parmesan cheese for garnish (optional)

1 In a large pot over medium-low heat, heat the olive oil. Add the carrots, celery, and onion and sauté, stirring occasionally until softened, about 7 minutes. Add the garlic and cook, stirring often, for 2 minutes.

2 Increase the heat to medium. Add the water, lentils, tomatoes, parsley, bay leaf, and thyme. Cover and bring to a boil.

3 Reduce the heat to medium-low. Simmer, partially covered, until the lentils are tender, about 35 to 45 minutes. Remove the bay leaf.

4 Puree in batches in a food processor or blender. Alternatively, if you have a hand blender, leave the soup in the pot and blend.

5 Season with salt and pepper to taste and reheat. Serve with grated Parmesan cheese on top or on the side.

Per Serving: *Calories 183.0; Protein 11.5g; Carbohydrates 28.9g; Dietary fiber 10.8g; Total fat 3.2g; Saturated fat 0.4g; Cholesterol 0mg; Sodium 309.9mg.*

Lentil Soup with Sausage and Potatoes

Legumes, vegetables, meat, and potatoes, this all-star soup's got everything — great taste, great body, and it's marvelously filling.

Serves: *8 to 10*

Level: *Easy*

Preparation time: *10 minutes*

Cooking time: *55 to 65 minutes*

Freezes well

2 tablespoons olive oil

1 medium celery stalk, chopped

1 medium onion, chopped

1 carrot, chopped

2 plump cloves garlic, minced

8 cups water

1 pound brown lentils, rinsed and picked over

2 medium potatoes, about 12 ounces, peeled and diced

3 tablespoons minced fresh parsley

1 bay leaf

1 teaspoon minced fresh oregano or ½ teaspoon dried oregano

1 teaspoon minced fresh thyme or ½ teaspoon dried thyme

4–6 ounces sausage, such as kielbasa or chorizo, sliced

Salt to taste, about ½–1 teaspoon

½ teaspoon black pepper

1 In a large pot over medium-low heat, heat the olive oil. Add the celery, onion, and carrot and sauté, stirring occasionally, until softened, about 10 minutes. Add the garlic and cook, stirring often, for 2 minutes.

2 Increase the heat to medium. Add the water, lentils, potatoes, parsley, bay leaf, oregano, and thyme. Cover and bring to a boil.

3 Reduce the heat to medium-low. Simmer, partially covered, until the potatoes and lentils are tender, about 35 to 45 minutes.

4 Remove the bay leaf. If you want a thicker soup, puree 2 cups of the mixture in a food processor or blender. Return the puree to the pot.

5 Add the sliced sausage and cook for 10 minutes. Season with salt and pepper.

Caution: *Cured, smoked, and salted meats, such as bacon, ham, ham hocks, or sausage, add a salty flavor to the soup when it is cooking. Take extra care when adding salt after the soup is finished.*

Per Serving: Calories 231.6; Protein 13.0g; Carbohydrates 32.2g; Dietary fiber 10.4g; Total fat 6.3g; Saturated fat 1.6g; Cholesterol 7.6mg; Sodium 257.9mg.

South-of-the-Border Black Bean Soup

This popular black bean soup has many versions throughout Central and South America and the Caribbean, particularly in Mexico, Cuba, and Brazil. Spicy and filling, this vegetarian rendition spiked with sherry is a hit no matter what the weather.

Serves: 8

Level: Easy

Special equipment: Food processor, blender, or hand blender

Soaking time: 2 hours to overnight

Preparation time: 15 minutes

Cooking time: 2¼ to 3 hours

Freezes well

2 tablespoons olive or vegetable oil	1 bay leaf
2 medium onions, chopped	1 pound black beans, picked over and soaked
1 green bell pepper, chopped	¼–⅓ cup dry sherry (optional)
4–5 plump cloves garlic, minced	Salt to taste, about 1½–2 teaspoons
2–3 jalapeno peppers, seeded and minced	¼–½ teaspoon crushed red chili flakes (optional)
¾ teaspoon ground cumin	Chopped scallions for garnish
9–10 cups water	Sour cream or nonfat sour cream for garnish

1 In a large pot over medium heat, heat the olive oil. Add the onions and bell pepper and sauté, stirring occasionally, until softened, about 7 minutes. Add the garlic, jalapeno, and cumin and cook, stirring occasionally, for 2 minutes.

2 Add the water, bay leaf, and beans. Bring to a boil. Reduce the heat to medium-low and simmer, partially covered, for 2 to 2½ hours or until the beans are tender. Skim off any foam that forms. Add more water if too much evaporates.

3 Puree half of the beans in a food processor or blender, or mash them in a bowl with a potato masher. Alternatively, if you have a hand blender, leave the soup in the pot and partially blend.

4 Return the pureed beans to the pot. Add the sherry and season with salt. Simmer, uncovered, for 10 to 15 minutes.

5 Taste and add the red chili flakes, if using. Serve with a dollop of sour cream and garnished with scallions.

Variation: For a hearty nonvegetarian soup, add ¼–⅓ pound sliced chorizo or andouille sausage to the soup after you add the sherry. Serve the soup over rice. You can also garnish the vegetarian version with homemade bacon bits.

Per Serving: Calories 225.3; Protein 12.5g; Carbohydrates 35.8g; Dietary fiber 12.5g; Total fat 4.3g; Saturated fat 0.7g; Cholesterol 0mg; Sodium 448.3mg.

Garlicky White Bean Soup

This fabulous dish, native to Italy and southern France, uses either home-cooked or canned beans. Serve it with plenty of country style bread for dunking. The recipe can easily be doubled.

Serves: *4 to 6*

Level: *Easy*

Special equipment: *Food processor, blender, or hand blender*

Preparation time: *15 minutes*

Cooking time: *30 to 35 minutes*

Freezes well

2 tablespoons olive oil

1 small onion, chopped

1 medium carrot, chopped

1 celery stalk, chopped

3–4 plump cloves garlic, minced

1½ teaspoons minced fresh rosemary or ¾ teaspoon dried rosemary

3½ cups chicken broth or water

3–3½ cups cooked white beans (if using dried, cook ½ pound; if using canned, drain and rinse two 16-ounce cans)

Salt to taste, about ½–¾ teaspoon

¼ teaspoon freshly ground black pepper

2 tablespoons chopped flat-leaf parsley

1 In a large pot over medium heat, heat the olive oil. Add the onion, carrot, and celery and sauté, stirring occasionally, until tender, about 10 minutes. Add the garlic and rosemary and cook, stirring often, for 2 minutes.

2 Add the chicken broth and beans. Cover and simmer for 20 to 25 minutes.

3 Strain the soup, reserving the broth. Puree the beans and vegetables in batches in a food processor or blender with approximately 1½ cups of the broth. Alternatively, if you have a hand blender, leave the soup in the pot and blend.

4 Return the puree, and enough reserved broth to make a creamy consistency, to the pot. Reheat over medium heat, stirring occasionally. Season with salt and pepper. Stir in the parsley right before serving.

Variation: *To turn this recipe into a thick puree to use as dip for bread or vegetables for hors d'oeuvres or as a side dish, add less broth, only about ⅓–½ cup after pureeing, and stir to make a thick, smooth dip. Drizzle with a small amount of extra virgin olive oil before serving.*

Per Serving: *Calories 200.6; Protein 9.8g; Carbohydrates 25.5g; Dietary fiber 6.4g; Total fat 7.2g; Saturated fat 1.3g; Cholesterol 2.9mg; Sodium 798.1mg.*

Chickpea and Sausage Soup

This tasty Mediterranean soup features canned chickpeas and spicy sausage. Use a good quality sausage for the best result.

Serves: *6*

Level: *Easy*

Preparation time: *15 minutes*

Cooking time: *40 minutes*

Freezes well

2 tablespoons olive oil

1 medium onion, sliced

1 medium carrot, sliced

1 celery stalk, sliced

2 plump cloves garlic, minced

1½ cups shredded green or Savoy cabbage

5 cups chicken broth

One 20-ounce can chickpeas, drained and rinsed

1 medium potato, peeled and diced

½ teaspoon Hungarian sweet paprika

½ teaspoon freshly ground black pepper

¼–⅓ pound spicy sausage such as chorizo, andouille, or kielbasa, sliced

Salt to taste, about ¼–½ teaspoon

1 In a large pot, over medium heat, heat the olive oil. Add the onion, carrot, and celery and sauté, stirring occasionally, until softened, about 7 minutes. Add garlic and cabbage and cook, stirring occasionally, for 2 to 3 minutes.

2 Add the chicken broth, chickpeas, potato, paprika, and pepper. Simmer, partially covered, until the potatoes and cabbage are tender, about 25 to 30 minutes.

3 Add the sausage and cook until it is heated through, about 5 minutes. Season with salt.

Cook's Fact: *Andouille is a hot Cajun sausage, and chorizo is the spicy sausage found in Mexico, Portugal, and southern Africa. Kielbasa is a milder but flavorful and garlicky sausage from Poland.*

Per Serving: *Calories 259.4; Protein 9.1g; Carbohydrates 19.7g; Dietary fiber 4.2g; Total fat 16.4g; Saturated fat 4.2g; Cholesterol 20.8mg; Sodium 1266mg.*

Poor Man's Pinto Bean Soup

This hearty and fragrantly spiced soup features the humble pinto bean and takes advantage of canned beans. It's incredibly easy and delicious and can be made in less than an hour. Pink or red beans can be substituted.

Serves: *6*

Level: *Easy*

Special equipment: *Food processor, blender, or hand blender*

Preparation time: *15 minutes*

Cooking time: *35 to 45 minutes*

Freezes well

2 tablespoons olive oil	*Three 2-x-½-inch strips fresh lemon zest*
1 medium onion, chopped	*½ bay leaf*
1 medium carrot, chopped	*½ teaspoon ground allspice or mace*
1 celery stalk, chopped	*Salt to taste, about ¼–½ teaspoon*
2 plump cloves garlic, minced	*Freshly ground black pepper*
One 14-ounce can plum tomatoes with juice	*2 tablespoons chopped fresh cilantro or parsley*
2½ cups beef, chicken, or vegetable broth	*1–1½ teaspoons freshly grated lemon zest*
Two 16-ounce cans pinto beans, drained and rinsed, or 3 cups cooked pintos	*Tabasco on the side (optional)*

1 In a large pot over medium heat, heat the olive oil. Add the onion, carrot, and celery and sauté, stirring occasionally, until softened, about 10 minutes. Add the garlic and cook, stirring, for 1 minute.

2 Add the tomatoes, and break them up into pieces with the back of a wooden spoon. Add the broth, pinto beans, strips of lemon zest, bay leaf, and allspice. Reduce the heat to medium-low. Cover and simmer for 25 to 35 minutes.

3 With a slotted spoon, remove and discard the strips of lemon zest and the bay leaf. Remove half the solids from the pot and pulse in a food processor or blender with a small amount of the liquid until a chunky puree forms. Alternatively, if you have a hand blender, leave the soup in the pot and blend partially.

4 Return the puree to the reserved soup in the pot. Season with salt and pepper. Stir in the cilantro and grated lemon zest. Reheat over medium heat. Serve with Tabasco on the side.

Variation: *For a spicier version, add ½–1 seeded and minced jalapeño along with the garlic in step 1, or follow the recipe as written or add ¼–½ teaspoon crushed red chili flakes in Step 4, just before serving.*

Per Serving: *Calories 259.4; Protein 9.1g; Carbohydrates 19.7g; Dietary fiber 4.2g; Total fat 16.4g; Saturated fat 4.2g; Cholesterol 20.8mg; Sodium 1241mg.*

Chapter 9

Fresh Soup from the Garden

In This Chapter

▶ Discovering how to store and use the abundant produce available in the marketplace

▶ Creating garden variety soup recipes

*P*roduce is the essence of many fine soups, generating either a pleasingly straightforward taste or layers of subtle yet complex flavor. High-quality vegetables and fruit are fundamental to good cooking. Although most items are available year-round in supermarkets and specialty stores, items that are out of season can be lower in quality and more costly. Locally grown items are seasonal, and seasonal produce is what nearly always tastes best. How long vegetables last in your refrigerator depends on how fragile they are and how fresh they were when you bought them.

Price is a good indicator of what's in season. Tomatoes, for example, are more expensive in winter than in summer. Canned tomatoes or frozen veggies can be preferable when fresh isn't appealing or is beyond your budget. Try to purchase the freshest produce you can. Country farm stalls or city farmer's markets generally carry the cream of the crop, but many large groceries sell high-quality vegetables.

Seasonal produce summary

This convenient reference lets you know when it's prime time for a particular item, even those that are on the shelves throughout the year.

Spring and summer: asparagus, bell peppers, berries, corn, cucumbers, eggplant, garden peas, new potatoes, string and wax beans, sugar snap peas, snow peas, spinach, tomatoes, and zucchini

Fall and winter: acorn squash, butternut squash, apples, beets, broccoli, cabbage, carrots, cauliflower, leeks, onions, parsnips, pears, potatoes, pumpkins, rutabagas, sweet potatoes, and turnips

Year-round: bell peppers, carrots, celery, cantaloupe, lettuce, mushrooms, onions, potatoes, radishes, scallions, spinach, sweet potatoes

No matter when or where you buy them, it's important to select fresh, unblemished items with smooth, uncracked skin. However, when making soup, if some of your leftover veggies have a few dark patches or softer spots, you can cut them out. Of course, if the vegetables are rotten, moldy, smell strongly, or taste off, don't even think of using them. Throw them out.

Because vegetables are exposed to excessive handling and to pesticides, make sure that you clean produce well before you prepare it or eat it. Most vegetables and fruit can be washed in water, drained in a colander, and patted dry. Some root vegetables may require scrubbing with a brush and others, such as mushrooms and strawberries, are delicate and require only wiping with a clean damp cloth or a quick rinsing in cold water.

Too much moisture causes vegetables to decay, so don't wash produce before storing it in the refrigerator. Pat it dry if it's been misted in the store.

Most vegetables and some fruit, such as zucchini, bell peppers, carrots, apples, oranges, and lemons can be stored in a plastic bag in the crisper section of your refrigerator.

Vegetables and Fruit

You may want to explore a whole world of produce. These make great soups.

Apples and pears

These two fruits are delectable additions to many soups, both sweet and savory. Apples and pears come in numerous varieties. Select fruit that is firm and unblemished. For apples, I prefer to cook with Cortland, Granny Smith, Delicious, MacIntosh, and Rome; for pears, I prefer Bosc, Bartlett, or Anjou.

Both pears and apples should be peeled and cored before using in soup. Because the flesh turns brown, you may want to put the fruit in a bowl of acidulated water until you're ready to use it.

To make acidulated water, add a small amount of lemon juice or lime juice to a bowl of water. Put cut fruit such as apples and pears or vegetables such as artichokes in a bowl of acidulated water to keep the flesh from discoloring.

Asparagus

Choose firm spears that are uniform in size with tightly closed tips. Break off the bottom of the stalk where it bends; you shouldn't cut it with a knife. If the stems are large, make sure that you peel them to about ½ inch from the tip. Thin stalks rarely need peeling. Refrigerated, asparagus will keep for 3 to 5 days.

Grown in sandy soil, asparagus requires thorough washing. Soak it in a sink filled with cold water. Let it stand for several minutes, so the dirt sinks. Repeat the process until you're satisfied that it's clean.

Avocados

Native to tropical and subtropical climates, avocados were once called alligator pears. Haas avocados, with rough skin, have superior flavor, and I prefer them to their smooth-skinned counterpart, called Fuerte. A ripe avocado should give, but not be squishy, when you press on it. Buy avocados as you need them and store them at room temperature — 65 to 75 degrees F. If you have several that have ripened simultaneously, you can refrigerate them for a couple of days to keep them from becoming too soft.

To ripen hard avocados, put them in a sealed paper bag or wrap them in newspaper. In a day or two, they should be ripe.

Beans

Many kinds of beans exist, but in soups you will most often use ordinary string beans and lima beans. String beans should be bright green and firm and should snap when you break them. You can substitute wax beans for a change. Snap off the end of the bean where it was attached to the plant, not the tip. Beans can be sliced on an angle or in small pieces. Frozen string beans are just fine, but don't use canned, which lack texture and flavor.

Fresh lima beans are often hard to find, but if you are so fortunate, they should be medium sized in the pod, and the pod should snap crisply when broken. Fortunately, frozen lima beans are plentiful and can be used successfully in any recipe. You can choose whether to use regular or baby limas.

Beets

Beets are a sweet-tasting, ruby-colored root vegetable. If available, buy them with the leaves attached, but cut or twist off the tops before you store them in the refrigerator. (Save the tops to cook as greens.) They're also sold without tops and prepacked in bags. Fresh beets can last in your fridge for about 3 weeks. When beets are used in soup, they tend to dominate in flavor and turn any broth red. Cooked beets will discolor cutting boards and counters, so you should clean them before the stain sets.

Fresh beets are always cooked whole. In general, the cooking time for beets is as follows: 35 to 40 minutes for medium beets; 60 minutes or more for large beets.

To peel beets easily, cook them first, and then place them in a colander in the sink under cold running water or plunge them into a sink of cold water. Slice off the stem end of the beet. The skin should slip off easily if the beets are thoroughly cooked.

Beet greens can be cooked like spinach and served as a delightful and nutritious side dish. Uncooked, they will last about 3 days in your fridge.

Bell peppers

Look for a pepper with smooth skin that is firm when pressed gently. Green, red, and yellow peppers are available year round. Domestic bell peppers are generally less expensive than imported and are equally good. You can substitute red for yellow.

To prepare bell peppers, cut out the stem and remove the seeds. Slice the peppers in half lengthwise and trim off the inner membranes, then cut as directed.

Broccoli, cabbage, and cauliflower

All members of the cabbage family, these vegetables should be firm to the touch. Broccoli should have tight green florets and a rigid stem; cabbage should feel heavy for its size and have tight leaves; cauliflower should be off-white with little discoloration and have compact florets.

You can find several types of cabbage: green, red, Savoy, and Chinese or bok choy. Most of the soup recipes in this book call for green or Savoy. Some markets cut large cabbages into wedges. This is a good buy if you don't need much. Note, however, that cabbages can be kept in the refrigerator for 2 to 3 weeks.

When it comes to broccoli and cauliflower, try to purchase the whole piece of broccoli, with stems intact, or the entire head of cauliflower, instead of a few florets. The stems are quite flavorful and excellent for soup. Both can be stored in the refrigerator for about 5 days.

Separate broccoli and cauliflower into florets before washing.

Cantaloupes

American cantaloupes are actually muskmelons. They are low in calories, high in fiber, and an excellent source of vitamins A and C. A ripe cantaloupe should have a sweet and fruity, but not an overpowering aroma. The melon should yield slightly when pushed at the bottom end. The netting on the beige skin should be well raised. Store unripe melons at room temperature, but refrigerate ripe fruit and any leftovers.

Carrots and parsnips

Carrots are crunchy when raw and sweet when cooked. For soups, use full-size medium carrots, rather than baby carrots. Carrots can be refrigerated for 2 to 3 weeks. Avoid carrots that have a green tinge at the top, which indicates bitterness, and those that are cracked, which means they're old.

For those of you unaccustomed to parsnips, they are a long cream colored root that resembles a carrot. They should not be eaten raw. If the parsnips are large, the center of the stem may get woody, and it's best to cut out any tough core. They have a refrigerator life of 1 to 2 weeks.

Both of these root vegetables can be purchased in bags or in bundles with their leaves attached. Buying them with the tops attached is preferable, though you should cut off the tops and discard them before storing in your vegetable crisper.

Sometimes carrots and parsnips need to be scrubbed with a brush to remove dirt. After they are clean, peel them with a vegetable peeler.

Celery

Celery should be crisp and firm with leaves that show no signs of wilting. Some varieties are bright green, while others are a paler color. Pascal celery is the common green type that you may see advertised in grocery circulars. Ideally, celery should last about 2 weeks in the refrigerator; however, I find it often lasts less than that. If it's beginning to lose its firmness, it can still be used in soups, but it shouldn't be completely flexible.

Peeling the fibrous strings on large stalks with a vegetable peeler is a good idea.

Corn

Unless it's in season locally, I generally pass up so-called fresh corn. When fresh, it's the one vegetable I almost always insist on buying from a farmer's market or roadside stand. For the recipes in this book, you may choose white, yellow, or mixed yellow and white kernels. When you buy fresh corn, check for tight husks, corn silk that is toast colored at the top, and tightly packed, medium-size kernels. And of course, check for the dreaded wormholes. Do not buy prepacked sets of ears with the ends cut off or those that are partially husked because all the sweet, fresh flavor will be lost.

Frozen corn is also fine for any of the soup recipes in this book and is preferable to starchy or old so-called "fresh" corn. In a pinch, you can also use canned corn kernels that have been drained.

The sugar in corn turns to starch quickly. To keep it sweet, refrigerate it immediately after you buy it and try to cook it the same day. Husk the corn and remove the corn silk shortly before you're ready to cook it.

Cucumber

You'll find three types of cucumbers: waxy, English, and Kirby. Waxy cucumbers are medium sized and contain many seeds. English are long and narrow and have relatively few seeds. Usually, you'll find them wrapped in plastic. Both can be used in soups, as recipes indicate. The small Kirby cucumbers are for pickles and are generally not suitable for cooking. Cucumbers, when refrigerated, keep for about a week.

Eggplant

Eggplant, like the tomato, belongs to the nightshade family and is not actually classified as a vegetable, but as another fruit of the vine. Eggplant comes in familiar purple and less-known white, and either can be used for soup. Slender, purple Asian eggplant is also an option. Make sure that whichever variety you buy has a shiny skin and is firm to the touch with no soft spots. It should last about a week in the refrigerator. Eggplants are also called aubergines.

Greens: Swiss chard, spinach, escarole, and romaine

Look for leaves that are brightly colored without any discoloring spots or wilted edges. These greens can be very dirty and need to be washed well in a sink full of cold water — often, more than once. I usually wash them several times just to be sure, because gritty greens will spoil your soup. If you're using them for something other than soup, you should spin them dry in a salad spinner to keep them crisp.

Store cleaned, dried greens in a perforated plastic bag in the vegetable drawer of your refrigerator.

Leeks

Leeks are a member of the onion family, but have a milder, somewhat sweeter taste. They resemble large scallions and should be stored in the refrigerator. Try to choose leeks that are of similar size, sometimes a challenge, as many markets randomly bundle them. The white part should be firm to the touch and the greens should not be yellowed.

Leeks can be quite gritty. Dirt is often hidden and trapped between the layers. Cut the leeks first and then wash them.

Cutting leeks

Slice off the top green part and the root end and discard, as shown in Figure 9-1. Peel and discard any tough outer layers. For slices, cut the leek in half lengthwise, then slice crosswise into half-moons. For thin strips, cut the leek lengthwise, then into 2-inch pieces, and cut into thin strips.

ON A CUTTING BOARD, USING A
CHEF'S KNIFE, CUT OFF THE ROOT
ENDS OF THE LEEKS.

SLICE THE LEEK LENGTHWISE,
WITH THE TIP OF THE KNIFE.

Washing leeks

Swish sliced leeks in a bowl of cold water. Let them stand for a few minutes
so the dirt sinks to the bottom. Lift them out with a slotted spoon, skimmer,
or small sieve. You'll probably have to wash them more than once, using
fresh water each time.

Mushrooms

Fresh mushrooms are very perishable and should be used within a few days
of purchase. Buy those that are firm, without discolored spots or a slimy surface. Always store them in the refrigerator.

Knowing mushroom varieties

Many kinds of mushrooms are now available in supermarkets and green gro-
cers. Wild mushrooms have more character than their white counterpart,
and dried mushrooms have an even more intense flavor. This list and Figure
9-2 help you know what to buy:

- **White cultivated:** These mushrooms, sometimes called button mushrooms, are the common, everyday mushrooms you find in supermarket
  produce sections. Although mild in flavor, they are terrific in soup. Add a
  few wild mushrooms if you want a fuller mushroom taste.

- **Cremini:** This is a tan to light brown mushroom with a slightly stronger
  taste than ordinary white mushrooms.

- **Shiitake:** Now commercially grown, these Japanese mushrooms have a
  marvelously rich flavor. They're terrific in any mushroom dish, particularly soups. Do not use the stems because they impart an unpleasant

taste. Twist the stems off of the cap and discard them, then slice the cap into strips. Shiitakes are also available dried and should be reconstituted before using.

- ✔ **Porcini or cepes:** Highly flavorful, these wild mushrooms, native to Italy and France, as well as parts of North America, can be combined with white or cremini mushrooms in soups. They're often used dried and reconstituted. Although they may seem costly, they're worth it — a little goes a long way in terms of taste.

- ✔ **Chanterelles:** Another species of wild mushroom, chanterelles have a delicate taste and can be combined with other varieties in mushroom soups. They are also available dried.

- ✔ **Portabello:** Large and meaty, these mushrooms are best for grilling or sautéing, although you can add a chopped one to any mushroom soup.

- ✔ **Wood and cloud ear:** These dried Chinese mushrooms have a unique, earthy taste and must be reconstituted.

- ✔ **Morels:** These are 4-star mushrooms, incredibly tasty with an intense flavor. They should be reserved for sauces or sautéed with vegetables such asparagus. I wouldn't use them in soup.

- ✔ **Oyster:** These white, irregularly-shaped mushrooms have a very delicate taste. They can be combined with other mushrooms in soups and stir-fries. If dried, they should be reconstituted.

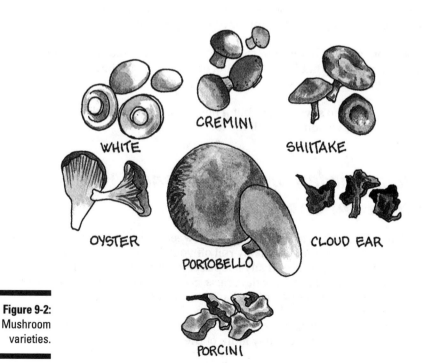

Figure 9-2:
Mushroom
varieties.

To clean mushrooms, wipe the stems with a damp cloth or paper towel. If the mushrooms are very dirty, swirl them quickly and gently in a sink filled with cool water and drain them immediately so their flavor won't be lost.

Using dried mushrooms

Generally 4 to 6 dried mushrooms will be adequate for boosting mushroom taste in soups. They must be reconstituted before you can use them. Put the mushrooms in a small bowl and pour boiling water over them. Let them stand for 20 to 30 minutes. Remove the mushrooms with a slotted spoon and chop or cut them. Instead of chopping reconstituted mushrooms, I find it easier to cut them into small pieces with scissors. It's just as effective.

Pour the mushroom soaking liquid through a sieve lined with a paper coffee filter to remove any grit. Use the mushroom soaking liquid in place of some of the broth. It will add a stronger mushroom flavor to the soup.

Onions

Onions, unlike their relatives, scallions and leeks, do not need to be refrigerated, but can be stored in a cool, dry place. I like to keep them in a wire basket so air circulates around them. Although you can find many kinds of onions — red, white, pearl, sweet Walla-Walla, and Vidalias, as well as large Spanish and Bermuda onions — the common yellow onion of medium size is preferable for soups unless another type is specified.

Choose onions that are firm to the touch and are covered with papery yellow skin. Avoid onions that have soft spots or a strong odor because they may be beginning to spoil.

Buying in bulk can save money, but if one onion is going bad, discard it immediately. One bad onion can spoil the lot.

Peas: Garden or English, snow peas, and sugar snap peas

Garden or English peas are the everyday sweet, round green peas that we eat shelled — the ones that invariably roll off your fork onto your lap. Frozen common peas are just fine in any soup recipe, but never use canned, which are mushy and comparatively flavorless. Snow peas and sugar snap peas are relatives, but the entire pod of both of these can be eaten. Remove the thin string that runs along the bottom of the pod before preparing them. Pods for any peas should be bright green and crisp. Peas will keep, refrigerated, for about 3 days, though every day more of the fresh sweet flavor is lost.

Substitute fresh sugar snap peas, which are sweeter, for snow peas in soup recipes if you want. When in season, they are less expensive.

Potatoes

Although potatoes come in endless varieties, from purple to gold, two main categories of potatoes exist: waxy or starchy. Waxy or all-purpose are the best kind for soup. These include Maine, Long Island, round red or white, and long white potatoes. The second category is starchy potatoes, such as Idaho and russet. Although excellent for baking, starchy potatoes will fall apart in soup. New potatoes aren't a different type of potato, but are simply potatoes that were harvested young and should be cooked soon after purchase.

Potatoes should be firm and without blemishes, cracks, or sprouts. You may need to scrub them with a brush to remove dirt. Store in a cool, dry place for up to 1 month, but don't refrigerate them. I keep mine in a basket so the air circulates freely around them.

Radishes

Most folks are familiar with the small, round, red radish, which is often used in salads. Daikon, a variety popular in Japan, is white and quite large, and it is sometimes sold in pieces. Purchase firm radishes and store them in the refrigerator for about a week.

Scallions

Most scallions, also known as spring onions or green onions, are young onions, although occasionally they can be immature leeks. They should be kept refrigerated. Select scallions with a firm white end and bright green tops.

To cut a scallion, trim a couple inches from the greens, even if you're going to use these for garnish, and cut off the root end. With the tip of a paring knife, loosen and peel any tough outer layers. If you're using only the white part, trim to just where the stem begins to turn bright green. Slice into thin pieces or chunks as called for in the recipe.

Squash

Squash comes in two varieties: winter and summer. Winter squashes include butternut, pumpkin, Hubbard, acorn, and spaghetti squash. Summer squashes include zucchini and crookneck, also known as yellow squash. All varieties, except spaghetti squash, make terrific soup.

Winter squash can be kept unrefrigerated in a cool, dry place for several months. The tough outer skin must be peeled before steaming or boiling, but should be left intact for baking. One way to prepare winter squash for soup or a side dish is to peel it, cut it in half lengthwise and scoop out the seeds, then cut it into evenly sized cubes, about 1½ to 2 inches. The squash is ready to be cooked until it's tender by steaming or simmering. You may also cook it in the microwave. After it's cooked, it can be pureed. Another method is to slice it in half lengthwise, take out the seeds, and place it skin-side up in a glass baking dish. Bake in a 350-degree-F oven or in the microwave until very tender. Scoop out the soft pulp and puree.

Summer squash should be firm to the touch. In soups, it can be sliced, diced, or cut into half-moons or thin strips. It requires no peeling and can last about 4 to 5 days in the refrigerator.

Sweet potatoes

Sweet potatoes are beautiful orange-fleshed potatoes with a delightfully sweet taste. Try to buy only what you will use, because they don't keep for long — only a couple of weeks if kept in a cool, dry, and dark place. Don't refrigerate them or their lovely texture will become mealy. Be adventurous and substitute sweet potatoes occasionally for regular potatoes in the soup recipes.

In the U.S., sweet potatoes are sometimes called yams, but this is a misnomer. Real yams aren't kin to sweet potatoes.

Tomatoes

Tomatoes come in two varieties: plum or Italian tomatoes that have an oval or teardrop shape and ordinary round tomatoes (see Figure 9-3). Plum tomatoes are sweeter and meatier. Round tomatoes come in several sizes from cherry to beefsteak and also are available in a range of colors from red to pink to yellow. Tomatoes have the best flavor when left at room temperature, however if you plan to keep ripe ones more than a few days, they can be refrigerated for a day or two to prevent them from ripening further. Fresh tomatoes can be kept at room temperature for 3 to 5 days.

For the soup recipes, choose firm, ripe, red tomatoes, either plum or round and medium in size. In winter, plum tomatoes often have superior taste to round, unless you buy those that are imported from Holland or Israel or hydroponically grown. These are always more expensive.

Figure 9-3:
Tomato
types.

PLUM   ROUND

Canned tomatoes are preferably to pithy, unripe tomatoes. They are economical and convenient, and they work well in most soup recipes. They're already peeled.

If recipes call for peeled, seeded tomatoes, peel them first, and then seed them, reserving the juice if you want to add it to the soup.

Peeling a tomato

In a saucepan, bring water to a boil. With a paring knife, lightly cut an X in the skin on the bottom of a whole tomato without piercing its flesh. Immerse the tomato in the boiling water for 15 to 30 seconds. With a slotted spoon or sieve, remove the tomato and set it aside. If you leave the tomato in the boiling water longer than 30 seconds, plunge it into a bowl of ice water to stop the cooking. Peel the skin off with the tip of the paring knife. It should slip right off.

Seeding a tomato

Slice the tomato lengthwise from top to bottom and cut out the core at the top. Flick the seeds out with your finger. If you want to reserve the juice, gently squeeze the tomato over a sieve set in a bowl, and then flick out the seeds with your finger.

Turnips and rutabagas

Turnips are round or oval, white-fleshed roots with purple tinged tops. Their larger relatives rutabagas (also known as Swedish turnips or Swedes) have yellow flesh with similar purple markings and are sometimes coated with wax. Both need to be washed and peeled. Use them interchangeably.

Garden Variety Soups

When it comes to soup, vegetables, which are often bit players in other dishes, can take top billing. They form the basis for an infinite array of appealing combinations and variations.

Curried Zucchini Soup

This remarkably easy recipe turns zucchini into a delightfully spiced soup. This soup is just as tasty if served cold. Add the cream, cool the soup, chill in the refrigerator for 1½ to 2 hours, then garnish and serve.

Yield: 6 servings

Level: Easy

Tools: Food processor, blender, or hand blender

Preparation time: 10 minutes

Cooking time: 35 to 45 minutes

Freezes well

2 tablespoons butter or margarine	*4 cups chicken or vegetable broth*
1 small onion, chopped	*Salt to taste (start with about ¾ teaspoon)*
1 plump clove garlic, minced	*½ cup cream or half-and-half (optional)*
2 teaspoons good quality curry powder (preferably Madras)	*fresh chopped mint leaves or chopped chives for garnish*
2 pounds, about 5 to 6, small zucchini, sliced	

1 In a large pot over medium-low heat, melt the butter. Add the onion and sauté, stirring occasionally, until translucent, about 5 to 7 minutes. Add the garlic and curry powder and sauté, stirring occasionally, for 2 minutes.

2 Add the chicken broth and zucchini. Cover partially and simmer until the zucchini is very tender, about 20 to 25 minutes.

3 Puree the mixture in batches in a food processor or blender. Alternatively, if you have a hand blender, leave the soup in the pot and blend.

4 Taste, season with salt, and stir in the cream (if desired). Return the mixture to the pot and heat thoroughly over medium heat for about 5 to 10 minutes. Serve garnished with mint or chives.

Per Serving: Calories 85.7; Protein 1.7g; Carbohydrates 6.0g; Dietary fiber 2.1g; Total fat 6.7g; Saturated fat 3.1g; Cholesterol 13.7mg; Sodium 1058.4mg.

Sweet Potato Bisque

Sweet potatoes, lightly scented with cinnamon and cloves, are the star of this unusual and lovely soup.

Yield: *6 to 8 servings*

Level: *Easy*

Preparation time: *1 hour*

Cooking time: *10 to 15 minutes*

Freezes well

3 pounds sweet potatoes	*¼ teaspoon ground white pepper*
2 tablespoons butter	*⅛ teaspoon ground cloves or allspice*
⅓ cup orange juice	*2 ½ cups chicken broth*
2 tablespoons brown sugar	*½ cup milk, half-and-half, or cream*
½ teaspoon cinnamon	*Salt to taste*

1 Preheat the oven to 400 degrees F. Prick the sweet potatoes with a knife. Bake them for 50 to 60 minutes or until the potatoes are cooked through and can be pierced easily with a paring knife.

2 Halve the potatoes and scoop out the pulp, discarding the skins. Press the sweet potato pulp through a potato ricer or a food mill into a large bowl, or place the flesh in a large bowl and mash it thoroughly with a potato masher.

3 Add the butter, orange juice, brown sugar, cinnamon, pepper, and ground cloves. Stir until smooth. You should have about 4 cups of mashed sweet potatoes.

4 In a large pot, combine the potatoes, broth, and milk and heat thoroughly over medium heat for about 5 to 10 minutes. Thin with additional juice or milk if necessary. Season with salt. Serve garnished with chives.

Tip: If you're already baking sweet potatoes, add a few extra and mash them with seasonings as directed. Cover and store the mashed sweet potatoes in the refrigerator. Complete the soup the following day by combining the potatoes with the broth and milk.

Per Serving: Calories 172.1; Protein 2.7g; Carbohydrates 30.4g; Dietary fiber 3.2g; Total fat 4.8g; Saturated fat 2.4g; Cholesterol 11.4mg; Sodium 405.0mg.

Turnip Apple Soup

Turnip soup? Why not! Turnips, mellowed with apples, make one absolutely stunning soup.

Golden Delicious apples are called for in this recipe, but you can substitute other sweet apples such as Red Delicious, Cortland, or Rome. Rome apples are wonderfully flavorful, but are sometimes almost twice the size of other apples — you might only need one of these.

Yield: *6 servings*

Level: *Easy*

Tools: *Food processor or blender*

Preparation time: *10 to 15 minutes*

Cooking time: *45 to 55 minutes*

Freezes well

1¼ pounds white turnips or rutabagas, peeled and cut into 1½ inch chunks

2 tablespoons butter

1 small onion, chopped

2 medium Golden Delicious apples, peeled, cored, and chopped

1 small onion, chopped

1 tablespoon sugar

¼ teaspoon cinnamon

⅛ teaspoon freshly grated nutmeg

3 cups chicken broth

½ cup half-and-half, milk, or apple cider

Salt to taste, about ¾ teaspoon

1 Put the turnips in a large saucepan and cover them with plenty of cold water. Over medium-high heat, bring to a boil and boil until the turnips can be pierced easily with a fork and are very tender, about 10 to 15 minutes. Drain well in a colander.

2 Meanwhile, in a small skillet over medium heat, melt the butter. Add the onion and apples and sauté, stirring occasionally, until very tender, about 10 to 15 minutes. Add the sugar, cinnamon, and nutmeg and cook, stirring occasionally, for 5 minutes.

3 Puree the turnips and apple-onion mixture in a food processor or blender until smooth. Add a little broth if necessary.

4 Transfer the puree to a large pot. Add the chicken broth, half-and-half, and salt to taste. Heat over medium heat until hot, about 10 minutes. Thin with extra broth if necessary when reheating.

Per Serving: *Calories 134.5; Protein 1.9g; Carbohydrates 14.4g; Dietary fiber 2.8g; Total fat 8.4g; Saturated fat 4.4g; Cholesterol 20.3mg; Sodium 844.1mg.*

Spiced Butternut Apple Soup

A fall and winter classic in my kitchen, this warming soup is a delightful blend of butternut squash, apples, cinnamon, and curry.

Yield: *6 servings*

Level: *Easy*

Tools: *Food processor, blender, or hand blender*

Preparation time: *10 to 15*

Cooking time: *40 to 45 minutes*

Freezes well

2 tablespoons butter or margarine

2 medium onions, chopped

1 cinnamon stick

1 bay leaf

1½ tablespoons good quality curry powder (preferably Madras)

3 cups chicken or vegetable broth

1¾ pounds butternut squash, peeled, seeded, and cut into 1½ inch chunks, about 3½ to 4 cups

2 medium Granny Smith apples, peeled, cored, and chopped

¾ cup apple cider or apple juice

Salt to taste, about ¾ to 1 teaspoon

1 In a large pot over medium-low heat, melt the butter. Add the onions, cinnamon stick, and bay leaf and sauté, stirring often, until translucent, about 5 to 7 minutes. Add the curry powder and cook, stirring often, for 2 minutes.

2 Add the chicken broth, butternut, and apples and simmer, partially covered, until tender, about 20 to 25 minutes. Remove the bay leaf and cinnamon stick.

3 With a slotted spoon, transfer the butternut, apples, and onions to a food processor, but leave the broth in the pot. Puree until smooth. Alternatively, if you have a hand blender, leave the soup in the pot and blend.

4 Return the puree and reserved broth to the pot. Add the apple cider and salt and stir to blend. Heat thoroughly over medium heat for 5 to 10 minutes. If the soup is too thick, thin with extra apple cider.

Cook's Fact: *Butternut, like other winter squash such as acorn or Hubbard, are good sources of vitamins A and C and iron. Feel free to try other winter squash in this soup.*

Per Serving: *Calories 158.5; Protein 2.2g; Carbohydrates 26.3g; Dietary fiber 5.6g; Total fat 6.3g; Saturated fat 3.0g; Cholesterol 12.9mg; Sodium 799.9mg.*

Roasted Red or Yellow Pepper Soup

Roasted bell peppers make a splendid soup. Roasting not only removes the skin, but also softens the flesh and intensifies the sweetness of the peppers.

Yield: *4 to 6 servings*

Level: *Intermediate to challenging*

Tools: *Food processor, blender, or hand blender*

Preparation time: *30 minutes*

Cooking time: *60 minutes*

Freezes well

6 red or yellow bell peppers, seeded and halved	*3 ½ cups chicken or vegetable broth*
2 tablespoons olive oil, plus additional for rubbing the peppers	*1 ½ teaspoons chopped fresh rosemary, or ¾ teaspoon dried rosemary*
1 medium onion, chopped	*Salt to taste, about ½ to ¾ teaspoon*
1 small celery stalk, finely diced, about ⅓ cup	*¼ teaspoon freshly ground black pepper*
2 cups shredded carrots, about 3 to 4 medium	*⅛ teaspoon cayenne (optional)*
1 plump clove garlic, minced	*2 teaspoons fresh lemon juice*
⅔ cup dry white wine or vermouth	*¼ cup sour cream for garnish (optional)*

1 To roast the peppers: Preheat the broiler. Flatten the peppers slightly. Lightly rub them with some olive oil, put them skin side up on a broiler tray or baking sheet, and broil until the skins are blistered and charred. Put the peppers in a paper or plastic bag and close tightly. When the peppers are cool enough to handle, peel, using a paring knife to scrape off the skin and discard it. Slice the peppers thinly.

2 In a large pot over medium heat, heat the olive oil. Add the onion and celery. Sauté, stirring occasionally, until very tender, about 15 minutes. Add the carrots and garlic and sauté, stirring occasionally, for 5 minutes. Add the white wine and cook for 3 minutes.

3 Add the broth, peppers, and rosemary. Reduce the heat to medium-low. Cover and simmer until the vegetables are very tender, about 30 minutes.

4 Strain the soup, reserving the broth. Puree the vegetables with a small amount of the broth in batches in a food processor or blender until smooth. Alternatively, if you have a hand blender, leave the soup in the pot, but remove some of the broth and blend.

5 Combine the puree with enough of the reserved broth to make the desired consistency. Season with salt, pepper, cayenne (if desired), and lemon juice. Reheat over medium heat. Swirl in the cream or sour cream (if desired).

Per Serving: Calories 121.1; Protein 2.3g; Carbohydrates 13.4g; Dietary fiber 3.9g; Total fat 7.2g; Saturated fat 1.2g; Cholesterol 2.9mg; Sodium 800.8mg.

Thrifty French Housewife's Soup

Traditionally named for women who are noted for their skill and frugality in the kitchen, other titles for this recipe could be "Nothing's in the Fridge Soup" or "Don't Get Paid 'Til Friday Soup." It's inexpensive, easy, and always good.

Yield: *6 servings*

Level: *Easy*

Tools: *Food processor, blender, or hand blender*

Preparation time: *10 to 15 minutes*

Cooking time: *55 to 65 minutes*

Freezes well

3 tablespoons butter or margarine

2 medium onions, thinly sliced

2 celery stalks, chopped

1 large or 2 medium carrots, chopped

½ teaspoon minced fresh thyme leaves, or ¼ teaspoon dried thyme

5 cups chicken or vegetable broth

¾ pounds potatoes, about 2 medium, peeled and thinly sliced

½ cup chopped parsley

Salt to taste, about ½ to ¾ teaspoon

Freshly ground black pepper to taste

1 In a large pot over medium heat, melt the butter. Add the onion, celery, carrot, and thyme and sauté, stirring occasionally, until softened, about 10 to 15 minutes.

2 Add the chicken broth, potatoes, and parsley. Cook, partially covered, until the vegetables are very tender, 35 to 45 minutes.

3 Puree in batches in a food processor or blender until smooth. Alternatively, if you have a hand blender, leave the soup in the pot and blend.

4 Return the soup to the pot. Thin with additional broth, water, or milk if necessary. Taste and season with salt and pepper. Heat thoroughly over medium heat for 5 to 10 minutes.

Variation: *Add a few leftover cooked vegetables such as green beans, peas, or broccoli in Step 2. You'll need to thin the soup with additional broth.*

Per Serving: *Calories 148.6; Protein 2.5g; Carbohydrates 14.9g; Dietary fiber 2.2g; Total fat 9.2g; Saturated fat 4.4g; Cholesterol 19.7mg; Sodium 1056.5mg.*

Herbed Beet Soup

A variation of borscht, this smooth ruby-colored, pureed soup is truly a masterpiece. It can be made with fresh cooked or canned beets and is excellent hot or cold.

Yield: *4 to 6 servings*

Level: *Easy*

Tools: *Food processor, blender, or hand blender*

Preparation time: *10 minutes plus 35 to 45 minutes beet cooking time*

Cooking time: *30 to 35 minutes*

Freezes well

2 tablespoons butter or margarine

1 medium onion, chopped

1½ tablespoons all-purpose flour

3 cups chicken broth

1 pound (3 to 4 medium) beets, cooked, skinned, and sliced (or about 2 ½ to 3 cups if using canned, drained beets)

1 teaspoon minced fresh thyme, or ½ teaspoon dried thyme

¾ teaspoon minced fresh rosemary, or ¼ teaspoon dried rosemary

1½ teaspoons red wine vinegar or lemon juice

½ teaspoon Dijon mustard

Salt to taste

½ cup sour cream, nonfat sour cream, or yogurt for garnish

Chopped fresh chives or snipped fresh dill for garnish

1 In a large pot over medium-low heat, melt the butter. Add the onion and sauté, stirring occasionally, until translucent, about 5 minutes.

2 Add the flour and cook, stirring constantly, for 3 to 5 minutes. Add the chicken broth.

3 Increase the heat to medium and cook until the broth thickens slightly, about 5 minutes.

4 Add the cooked beets, thyme, rosemary, wine vinegar, and mustard. Simmer, partially covered, for 10 to 15 minutes.

5 Puree in batches in a food processor or blender until smooth. Alternatively, if you have a hand blender, leave the soup in the pot and blend.

6 Return the soup to the pot. Thin with additional broth if necessary. Reduce the heat to medium-low and reheat thoroughly. Taste and season with salt. Serve garnished with sour cream and chives.

Variation: *This soup can also be served cold. After pureeing, chill thoroughly, about 1½ to 2 hours. Garnish and serve.*

Per Serving: *Calories 97.6; Protein 2.1g; Carbohydrates 9.7g; Dietary fiber 1.7g; Total fat 6.0g; Saturated fat 2.9g; Cholesterol 12.9mg; Sodium 662mg.*

Fresh Tomato Basil Soup

Tomato and basil are perfect partners in everything, from pasta sauces to this superb soup. This soup is best in the summer when tomatoes are at their peak. During winter months, use plum tomatoes or costly ripe, imported tomatoes.

Yield: *4 to 6 servings*

Level: *Easy*

Tools: *Food processor, blender, or hand blender*

Preparation time: *15 minutes*

Cooking time: *40 minutes*

Freezes well

2 tablespoons olive oil

1 medium onion, chopped

1 plump clove garlic, minced

3 ½ pounds ripe, fresh tomatoes, peeled, seeded, and coarsely chopped with juices

½ bay leaf

1 cup vegetable or chicken broth

Salt to taste, about ½ to 1 teaspoon

¼ teaspoon freshly ground black pepper

2 tablespoons minced fresh basil or prepared pesto

1 In a large pot over medium heat, heat the olive oil. Add the onion and sauté, stirring occasionally, until the onion is tender and golden, about 10 minutes. Add the garlic and cook, stirring, for 1 minute.

2 Add the tomatoes and bay leaf, cover, and simmer until the tomatoes are very soft, about 30 minutes.

3 Remove the bay leaf. Puree in batches in a food processor until smooth. Alternatively, if you have a hand blender, leave the soup in the pot and blend.

4 Return the soup to the pot. Add the broth, and reheat until hot. Season with salt and pepper. Stir in the basil or pesto before serving.

Cook's Fact: *Tomatoes originated in South America and were transported from the New World to Europe by the Spanish. The French, believing this fruit of the vine was an aphrodisiac, called them pommes d'amour or love apples.*

Per Serving: *Calories 105.0; Protein 2.8g; Carbohydrates 14.2g; Dietary fiber 3.2g; Total fat 5.6g; Saturated fat 0.7g; Cholesterol 0mg; Sodium 384.8mg.*

Savory Tomato-Vegetable-Rice Soup

This herb-infused tomato-based soup accented by vegetables and rice is a pleasing alternative to broth-based vegetable soups.

You can substitute other vegetables, such as diced yellow squash and sliced green beans, for the zucchini and peas.

Yield: *6 to 8 servings*

Level: *Easy to Intermediate*

Preparation time: *10 to 15 minutes*

Cooking time: *50 to 60 minutes*

Freezes well

For the bouquet garni

1 bay leaf

2 small to medium sprigs fresh thyme, or ½ teaspoon dried thyme

3 to 4 sprigs parsley

3 black peppercorns

2 whole cloves

For the soup

2 tablespoons olive oil

1 medium onion, chopped

1 small carrot, finely diced

1 small celery stalk, finely diced

3 ½ cups chicken broth

2 ½ cups fresh or canned tomato puree

¼ cup white rice

1 medium zucchini or 2 baby zucchini, cut into half moons

3 to 4 teaspoons sugar or to taste

⅔ cup frozen or fresh peas

Salt to taste, about ½ to 1 teaspoon

¼ teaspoon freshly ground black pepper or to taste

2 tablespoons chopped fresh flat-leaf parsley

1 Prepare the bouquet garni by wrapping the ingredients in a small piece of cheesecloth and tying it to secure. Set aside.

2 In a large pot over medium-low heat, heat the olive oil. Add the onion, carrot, and celery and sauté, stirring occasionally, until tender, about 15 minutes.

3 Add the broth, tomato puree, rice, zucchini, sugar, and bouquet garni. Cover partially and simmer for 30 to 35 minutes. Add the peas and simmer, uncovered, for 5 to 10 minutes or until the peas are cooked through.

4 Remove the bouquet garni and discard. Season with salt and pepper. Stir in the parsley.

Per Serving: *Calories 130.9; Protein 3.4g; Carbohydrates 18.9g; Dietary fiber 3.2g; Total fat 5.4g; Saturated fat 0.9g; Cholesterol 2.2mg; Sodium 633.4mg.*

Lettuce and Herb Soup

I prefer to use romaine in this soup, but feel free to try other green lettuce varieties — anything except iceberg, which is too watery and flavorless.

Yield: *4 to 6 servings*

Level: *Intermediate*

Tools: *Food processor, blender, or hand blender*

Preparation time: *10 minutes*

Cooking time: *15 minutes*

Freezes well

1 tablespoon butter or margarine

6 scallions, white part only, thinly sliced

3 cups vegetable or chicken broth

8 cups chopped romaine lettuce

2 tablespoons chopped parsley

2 tablespoons minced fresh herbs: any combination of basil, chervil, thyme, chives, or celery leaves

1⅓ cups half-and-half or milk

1 egg yolk

Salt to taste, about ½ to ¾ teaspoon

Freshly ground black pepper

Freshly grated Romano or Parmesan cheese for garnish (optional)

1 In a large pot over medium heat, melt the butter. Add the scallions and sauté, stirring occasionally, until softened, about 3 minutes.

2 Add the broth and bring to a boil. Add the lettuce, cover, and simmer until the lettuce is wilted, about 3 to 5 minutes.

3 Add the parsley and mixed herbs. Puree the mixture in batches in a food processor or blender. Alternatively if you have a hand blender, leave the soup in the pot and blend.

4 Return the mixture to the pot and reheat over medium-low heat.

5 In a small bowl, lightly whisk together the half-and-half and egg yolk. While whisking constantly, add a little heated soup to the egg mixture. Continue to whisk constantly as you pour the egg mixture into the soup in a steady stream. Simmer gently over medium-low heat until the soup thickens slightly. Do not let the soup boil. Season with salt and freshly ground black pepper. Serve with Romano cheese on the side.

Cook's Fact: *Romaine, also known as Cos lettuce, is reportedly native to the island of Cos in the Aegean Sea. This crisp and flavorful green is the primary ingredient in ever-popular Caesar salad.*

Per Serving: *Calories 120.4; Protein 4.5g; Carbohydrates 6.3g; Dietary fiber 1.5g; Total fat 9.6g; Saturated fat 5.3g; Cholesterol 60.4mg; Sodium 724.8mg.*

Produce-buying tips

Produce that's in season is cheaper and has the best flavor. Select produce with a smooth, unblemished skin. Vegetables should be firm to the touch, whereas fruit should be ripe. If the fruit is not quite ripe, make sure it will have enough time to ripen before you plan to use it. Buy in bulk only those that you use often.

Frozen vegetables are good for soups when fresh are too expensive or out of season. If you don't have fresh vegetables, frozen are nearly always preferable to canned.

Parsnip and Blue Cheese Soup

Parsnips can hold their own in the presence of strongly flavored blue cheese, and the two blend harmoniously in this unique soup.

Yield: *6 servings*

Level: *Intermediate*

Tools: *Food processor, blender, or hand blender*

Preparation time: *15 minutes*

Cooking time: *40 to 45 minutes*

Do not freeze

For the bouquet garni

1 bay leaf

2 whole cloves

1 sprig thyme

3 sprigs parsley

For the soup

3 parsley stems

2 tablespoons butter or margarine

1 medium onion, chopped

1 plump clove garlic, minced

4 ½ cups chicken or vegetable broth

1 pound parsnips, peeled and diced, woody cores removed

1 medium potato, about 8 ounces, diced

1½ cups half-and-half, cream, or milk

½ cup crumbled blue cheese

¼ cup freshly ground Parmesan cheese

2 tablespoons chopped chives

1 Prepare the bouquet garni by wrapping the ingredients in a small piece of cheesecloth and tying it to secure. Set aside.

2 In a large pot over medium heat, melt the butter. Add the onion and sauté, stirring occasionally, until translucent, about 5 minutes. Add the garlic and cook, stirring often, for 1 to 2 minutes.

3 Add the broth, parsnips, potatoes, and bouquet garni and bring to a boil. Reduce the heat to medium-low. Cover and simmer until tender, about 30 to 35 minutes. Remove the bouquet garni and discard.

4 Use a slotted spoon to lift the solids into a bowl, leaving the broth in the pot. In a food processor or blender, puree the vegetables in batches with a small amount of the broth until smooth, returning each pureed batch to the pot. Alternatively, if you have a hand blender, leave the soup in the pot and blend.

5 Return the broth and the puree to the pot, and reheat over medium-low heat. The soup can be made ahead to this point.

6 In a small saucepan over medium-low heat, heat the half-and-half. Add the blue cheese and Parmesan, and stir constantly until the cheese is melted.

7 Pour the cheese mixture into the soup and stir to blend. Thin if necessary with extra broth or half-and-half. Serve immediately garnished with chopped chives. To reheat this soup, do so over medium-low heat, stirring frequently.

Variation: *Parsnips and carrots are perfect companions. For a colorful variation, use ½ pound parsnips and ½ pound carrots in this soup.*

Per Serving: *Calories 300.0; Protein 8.6g; Carbohydrates 26.4g; Dietary fiber 4.0g; Total fat 18.6g; Saturated fat 10.4g; Cholesterol 48.2mg; Sodium 1018.7mg.*

Eggplant and Garlic Soup

Eggplant, enhanced by garlic, is transformed into an elegant and smooth soup. It's excellent as a light meal or starter.

Yield: *6 servings*

Level: *Easy*

Tools: *Food processor, blender, or hand blender*

Preparation time: *10 to 15 minutes*

Cooking time: *50 to 60 minutes*

Freezes well

3 tablespoons olive oil

1 medium onion, chopped

1¼ pounds eggplant, peeled and diced

6 plump cloves garlic, minced, about 1 tablespoon

½ teaspoon ground cumin

½ teaspoon turmeric

4 cups vegetable or chicken broth

1 small potato, peeled and diced

Salt to taste, about ¾ teaspoon

¼ teaspoon freshly ground white pepper

¼ teaspoon ground cayenne

Fresh chopped cilantro for garnish

1 In a large pot over medium heat, heat 1 tablespoon of the olive oil. Add the onion and sauté, stirring occasionally, until translucent, about 5 minutes.

2 Add the remaining 2 tablespoons of olive oil and heat. Add the eggplant, garlic, cumin, and turmeric. Sauté, stirring occasionally, until softened, about 5 to 7 minutes.

3 Add the broth and potato. Reduce the heat to medium-low. Cover and simmer until the vegetables are very tender, about 30 to 40 minutes.

4 Puree in batches in a food processor or blender until smooth. Alternatively, if you have a hand blender, leave the soup in the pot and blend.

5 Reheat over medium heat, stirring occasionally. Thin with additional broth if necessary. Season with salt, white pepper, and cayenne. Garnish with cilantro.

Per Serving: *Calories 123.7; Protein 2.8g; Carbohydrates 13.7g; Dietary fiber 3.0g; Total fat 7.7g; Saturated fat 1.0g; Cholesterol 0mg; Sodium 962.2mg.*

Wild Rice and Mushroom Soup

The nutty taste of wild rice is outstanding with mushrooms. Try to include some wild mushrooms such as shiitakes (without their woody stems, please!), which are readily available fresh in many supermarkets.

Yield: *6 to 8 servings*

Level: *Easy*

Preparation time: *10 minutes*

Cooking time: *70 to 80 minutes*

Freezes well

½ cup wild or brown rice

2 tablespoons vegetable oil

6 scallions, white part only, minced

1 medium carrot, finely diced

1 stalk celery, finely diced, reserve 1 tablespoon minced celery leaves

¾ pound white, cremini, or shiitake mushrooms, or a combination, coarsely chopped

1 teaspoon minced fresh thyme leaves, or ½ teaspoon dried thyme

3 to 4 tablespoons dry sherry

6 cups chicken or vegetable broth

Salt to taste, about ½ teaspoon

¼ teaspoon freshly ground black pepper

2 tablespoons minced fresh parsley or chives

¼ to ½ cup cream (optional)

1 Wash the rice in a sieve under cold running water.

2 In a large pot over medium heat, heat the vegetable oil. Add the scallions, carrot, and celery and sauté, stirring occasionally, until tender, about 10 minutes. Add the mushrooms and thyme and cook, stirring occasionally, for 5 minutes.

3 Add the sherry and cook for 1 to 2 minutes. Add the broth and rice. Cover partially and simmer until the rice is tender, about 50 to 60 minutes.

4 Season with salt and pepper and stir in the reserved celery leaves and parsley. For a richer texture, add the cream.

Variation: **Mushroom Barley Soup:** *In winter, this hearty soup is a standard on many home and restaurant menus. Prepare the Wild Rice and Mushroom Soup above using white or cremini mushrooms. Substitute ⅓ cup pearl barley for the wild rice. Substitute 1 chopped medium onion for the scallions.*

Per Serving: Calories 116.2; Protein 3.3g; Carbohydrates 11.8g; Dietary fiber 1.9g; Total fat 6.7g; Saturated fat 1.0g; Cholesterol 3.8mg; Sodium 908.9mg.

Spring Vegetable Rice Soup

After a long winter, I love this especially light and fresh-tasting soup that hints of spring's arrival.

Yield: *6 to 8 servings*

Level: *Easy*

Preparation time: *15 minutes*

Cooking time: *35 to 40 minutes*

Freezes well

2 tablespoons olive oil

6 scallions, white part only, sliced

1 small carrot, shredded

1 small celery stalk, thinly sliced

1 plump clove garlic, minced

3 to 4 mushrooms, sliced

6 cups chicken or vegetable broth

⅓ cup white rice

1 medium tomato, peeled, seeded, and diced

1 small yellow squash, sliced

1 small zucchini, sliced

½ medium red or yellow bell pepper, cut into thin 1-inch strips, about ½ cup

¼ pound asparagus, trimmed and sliced or ½ cup sliced fresh green beans

3 tablespoons chopped fresh parsley

1 tablespoon minced fresh basil, dill, or chives

Salt to taste, about ½ teaspoon

Freshly ground black pepper to taste

1 In a large pot over medium heat, heat the olive oil. Add the scallions, carrot, and celery and sauté, stirring often, until the vegetables begin to soften, about 5 minutes. Add the garlic and mushrooms and cook, stirring, for 2 minutes.

2 Add the broth, rice, and tomato and bring to a boil. Reduce the heat to medium-low, cover, and cook until the rice is tender, about 15 to 20 minutes.

3 Add the yellow squash, zucchini, bell pepper, and asparagus and cook, uncovered, until the vegetables are just tender, about 7 to 10 minutes. Stir in the parsley and basil and season with salt and pepper.

Variation: *To make an even heartier meal, feel free to add 1 cup cooked (and shredded or diced) chicken or turkey when you add the squash and other vegetables.*

Per Serving: *Calories 113.7; Protein 2.7g; Carbohydrates 11.6g; Dietary fiber 1.9g; Total fat 6.6g; Saturated fat 1.3g; Cholesterol 3.8mg; Sodium 908.2mg.*

Cabbage and Bacon Soup

I like to make this soup in late autumn after the first frost, which causes cabbage to acquire a sweeter taste. I add a touch of caraway, but you may omit it if you don't like it.

Yield: *6 to 8 servings*

Level: *Easy*

Preparation time: *15 minutes*

Cooking time: *50 to 60 minutes*

Freezes well

6 strips bacon, sliced into small pieces or strips

2 tablespoons olive oil

1 medium onion, halved and thinly sliced

5 ½ cups cabbage

7 cups chicken broth

1 medium potato, peeled and diced

¼ to ½ teaspoon caraway seeds (optional)

Salt to taste, about ½ teaspoon

¼ teaspoon freshly ground black pepper

¼ cup minced fresh parsley

1 In a skillet over medium-low heat, cook the bacon until most of the fat is rendered. Remove the bacon with a slotted spoon and blot on a paper towel. Set aside.

2 In a large pot over medium-low heat, heat the olive oil. Add the onion and sauté, stirring occasionally, until the onion is almost golden, about 10 minutes. Add the bacon and cook for 5 minutes longer. Add the cabbage and cook, stirring occasionally, for 5 minutes.

3 Add the broth, potato, and caraway (if desired). Cover and simmer until the cabbage is very tender, 35 to 40 minutes. Season with salt and pepper. Stir in the parsley and serve immediately.

Tip: *To prepare the cabbage for this soup, remove any wilted outer leaves, cut out and discard the tough core, and cut the cabbage into wedges. Slice into thin strips. Refrigerate unused wedges.*

Per Serving: *Calories 125.0; Protein 3.5g; Carbohydrates 7.4g; Dietary fiber 1.7g; Total fat 9.4g; Saturated fat 2.2g; Cholesterol 8.4mg; Sodium 1106.3mg.*

Much ado about garlic

Garlic has been the subject of much folklore. Throughout the ages, the pungent bulb has been credited with the magical and mystical powers to ward off vampires and evil spirits, as well as a reputation for many health-giving benefits. Its proponents claim that eating garlic promotes strength, longevity, and a healthy heart. It's also been billed as a remedy for the common cold and toothaches.

Nana's Mix and Match Vegetable Soup

This is the old-fashioned vegetable soup that grandmothers used to make. Change it according to your mood, what's in season, and what you have on hand. Use a combination of the vegetables listed below or a mixture of vegetables you like, except beets or red cabbage, which are too dominant in flavor and color to blend well in this soup.

This soup is also an ideal way to use last night's vegetables. Reduce the cooking time by a few minutes if you are using leftovers.

Yield: *6 to 8 servings*

Level: *Easy*

Preparation time: *15 to 20 minutes*

Cooking time: *35 to 40 minutes*

Freezes well

2 tablespoons vegetable or olive oil

1 medium onion, quartered and thinly sliced

1 medium carrot, diced

1 celery stalk, diced, 1 tablespoon of leaves chopped and reserved

1 plump clove garlic, minced (optional)

6 cups chicken, beef, or vegetable broth

2 1/2 to 3 cups total of vegetables from root veggies and other veggies

Salt to taste, about 1/2 teaspoon

Freshly ground black pepper to taste

2 tablespoons minced fresh parsley

Root veggies

1/2 cup chopped turnip or rutabaga

1/2 cup diced peeled potato

1/2 cup diced or sweet potato, about a 3-ounce potato

Other veggies

½ cup fresh or frozen corn kernels

½ cup fresh or frozen peas

½ cup fresh or frozen string beans

½ cup chopped green or Savoy cabbage

½ cup diced zucchini

½ cup diced yellow squash

½ cup canned tomatoes, chopped or stewed, drained

1 In a large pot over medium heat, heat the vegetable oil. Add the onion, carrot, and celery and sauté, stirring occasionally, until softened, about 10 minutes. Add the garlic and cook, stirring, for 1 minute.

2 Add the broth and any selections from the root veggies list. Cover and bring to a gentle boil. Cover partially and simmer until the vegetables are almost tender, about 10 to 15 minutes.

3 Add your choices from the other veggies list. Add more broth if you want to add more veggies than suggested or if the soup is too chunky for you. Simmer, uncovered, until the vegetables are tender, about 10 to 12 minutes.

4 Season with salt and pepper. Stir in the parsley and reserved celery leaves.

Per Serving: Calories 83.8; Protein 1.5g; Carbohydrates 5.4g; Dietary fiber 1.3g; Total fat 6.5g; Saturated fat 1.0g; Cholesterol 3.8mg; Sodium 916.5mg.

Smooth purees

Sometimes a food processor doesn't make a puree as finely textured as you'd like. Blenders, hand or immersion blenders, or old-fashioned food mills generally make a smoother puree. If you only have a food processor, to make a smoother and lighter soup, such as the Roasted Red Pepper Soup, after combining the puree and broth, strain the soup by placing a strainer over a bowl. Pour the soup through the strainer, pushing on the puree with the back of a wooden spoon. Discard any remains of the puree that are left in the strainer. Return the soup to the pot, add the cream or milk if using, reheat, and serve. This technique can also used for other soups when you'd like an especially creamy, velvety texture.

Corn Chowder

This filling corn soup can be prepared with yellow or white corn. Although fresh is best, it's still wonderful with frozen corn. If using fresh corn, add the cobs to the pot when you add the broth because they impart a more robust corn flavor. Remove and discard the cobs before pureeing.

Yield: *6 to 8 servings*

Level: *Easy*

Tools: *Food processor, blender, or hand blender*

Preparation time: *15 minutes*

Cooking time: *45 to 50 minutes*

Freezes well

4 slices bacon, coarsely chopped	2 medium potatoes, about 12 ounces, peeled and diced
1 medium onion, chopped	
¾ teaspoon chopped fresh thyme, or ¼ teaspoon dried thyme	2 tablespoons chopped fresh parsley
	Salt to taste, about ½ teaspoon
2 cups chicken broth	Freshly ground black pepper to taste
2 cups half-and-half or milk	Tabasco to taste
3½ cups fresh or frozen corn kernels	

1 In a large pot over medium heat, cook the bacon. After the bacon is cooked, drain off all but 2 tablespoons of the bacon fat.

2 Add the onion and cook, stirring occasionally, until the onion is lightly golden, about 10 minutes. Add the thyme and stir.

3 Add the broth, half-and-half, corn, potatoes, and parsley. Reduce the heat to medium-low. Cover partially and simmer until the corn and potatoes are tender, about 20 to 25 minutes.

4 Remove half the solids from the pot and pulse in a food processor or blender with a small amount of the liquid until a chunky puree forms. Alternatively, if you have a hand blender, leave the soup in the pot and blend partially.

5 Return the puree to the pot. Season with salt and pepper and reheat. Serve with Tabasco sauce on the side.

Per Serving: *Calories 250.2; Protein 6.2g; Carbohydrates 29.1g; Dietary fiber 2.8g; Total fat 13.7g; Saturated fat 6.6g; Cholesterol 29.3mg; Sodium 485.4mg.*

Jalapeño, Tomato, and Corn Chowder

This tangy soup is a wonderful alternative to the traditional milk-based corn chowder. It's lower in fat and calories, but has plenty of flavor.

Yield: *6 to 8 servings*

Level: *Easy*

Tools: *Food processor or blender*

Preparation time: *10 to 15 minutes*

Cooking time: *1 to 1¼ hours*

Freezes well

2 cups cooked fresh or thawed frozen corn kernels

⅓ cup half-and-half or milk

1½ tablespoons olive oil

1 medium onion, chopped

1 small green bell pepper, chopped

½ to 1 jalapeño, seeded and minced

2 plump cloves garlic, minced

¾ teaspoon ground cumin

1 tablespoon tomato paste

3 cups chicken or vegetable broth

One 14-ounce can chopped tomatoes with juice

1 medium potato, about 6 to 8 ounces, peeled and diced

Salt to taste, about ½ to ¾ teaspoon

⅛ teaspoon cayenne (optional)

3 tablespoons chopped fresh cilantro

1 In a food processor or blender, puree 1¼ cups corn kernels with the half-and-half and set aside.

2 In a large pot over medium heat, heat the olive oil. Add the onion and bell pepper and sauté, stirring occasionally, until the onion is translucent, about 5 minutes. Add the jalapeño, garlic, and cumin and cook, stirring constantly, for 1 to 2 minutes. Add the tomato paste and cook, stirring constantly, about 1 minute.

3 Add the chicken broth, tomatoes, reserved pureed corn, the remaining ¾ cup whole corn kernels, and potato. Cover and simmer for 40 to 45 minutes.

4 Add the salt, cayenne (if desired), and cilantro and serve.

Variation: *Replace the potato with a medium sweet potato, peeled and diced, for a colorful variation.*

Per Serving: *Calories 124.9; Protein 3.2g; Carbohydrates 19.2g; Dietary fiber 2.8g; Total fat 5.0g; Saturated fat 1.0g; Cholesterol 3.2mg; Sodium 598.8mg.*

Spicy Pumpkin and Corn Chowder

This is one terrific soup! I've used creative license, continuing the chowder (r)evolution, by adding pumpkin puree, another American staple, to corn chowder.

Cayenne intensifies the longer the soup is stored, so if you prepare it ahead or plan to freeze it, use a smaller amount of cayenne than called for, about ⅛ to ¼ teaspoon.

Yield: *6 to 8 servings*

Level: *Easy*

Tools: *Food processor or blender*

Preparation time: *10 to 15 minutes*

Cooking time: *35 to 45 minutes*

Freezes well

1 tablespoon butter or margarine

6 scallions, white part only, sliced (reserve chopped greens for garnish)

2 plump cloves garlic, minced

1 tablespoon minced fresh ginger, about 1-inch piece

2 cups chicken broth

2 cups canned pureed pumpkin or pureed cooked butternut squash

¼ to ½ teaspoon cayenne or to taste

2 cups frozen corn kernels

½ cup cream, half-and-half, or milk

Finely grated zest of 1 small to medium lemon

Salt to taste, about ½ to 1 teaspoon

Homemade bacon bits (optional)

1 In a large pot over medium-low heat, melt the butter. Add the scallions and sauté, stirring occasionally, until tender, about 5 to 7 minutes. Add the garlic and ginger and cook, stirring, for 1 minute.

2 Add the chicken broth, pumpkin, and cayenne. Increase the heat to medium. Simmer, partially covered, for 15 to 20 minutes.

3 Meanwhile, cook the corn kernels according to package directions. Drain off any liquid. Place the corn in a food processor or blender, add the cream, and pulse until a thick puree forms.

4 Add the corn puree to the pumpkin soup. Add the lemon zest and salt and stir to blend. Heat thoroughly over medium heat, about 5 to 10 minutes. Garnish with the reserved scallion greens and bacon bits (if desired).

Tip: *To make butternut puree, peel a 2-pound butternut squash. Cut in half, remove the seeds, and cube. Steam or boil the butternut, or cook it in the microwave, until tender. Puree in a food processor or blender until smooth, along with a very small amount of broth if necessary. Makes approximately 2 cups of puree.*

Per Serving: *Calories 142.4; Protein 3.1g; Carbohydrates 16.1g; Dietary fiber 3.9g; Total fat 8.5g; Saturated fat 4.7g; Cholesterol 25.5mg; Sodium 411.3mg.*

Chapter 10

Soup from the Dairy Case

. . . .

In This Chapter

▶ Understanding dairy products and tofu

▶ Creating cream soup recipes, both light and rich

. . . .

Many dairy products are used in soup to lend creaminess, to balance other ingredients, to improve texture, and to add a final accent or garnish. Most people don't have to completely shy away from dairy products, but they do need to learn to use dairy in moderation. Milk, cream, sour cream, cheese, and butter provide essential calcium and fats when used in small quantities. Low-fat milk, low-fat buttermilk, nonfat yogurt, and low-fat or nonfat sour cream offer the same nutritional benefits with significantly less fat than the original versions.

Butter and Margarine

I use butter in some recipes because of its delicately rich and unbeatable flavor. Butter comes in sticks or tubs, and it's labeled either salted or sweet (which means unsalted). I prefer sweet because its taste is purer and creamier, but use whichever you like. Butter lasts for 2 to 3 weeks in the refrigerator. You can buy it when it's on sale and freeze it. It can be frozen for up to a year.

Margarine, although it looks similar to butter, lacks its unique, characteristic flavor, and you do compromise taste by substituting it. However, feel free to use margarine if that's what you prefer. Margarine is not any healthier than butter — it's a hydrogenated fat, which some experts now believe actually raises cholesterol levels. Stick margarine has the same fat and calorie count as butter. Reduced fat margarine has some caloric advantage.

Cream, Half-and-Half, Milk, and Buttermilk

Some soup recipes call for these items interchangeably. The choice is up to you, relative to how creamy a texture or how rich a flavor you want the end product to have. Store them all in the refrigerator in sealed containers.

When choosing cream, use light cream, which usually has 20 percent fat. Heavy cream is used for whipping and contains nearly double the amount of fat. Half-and-half has 10 to 12 percent fat.

Whole milk has approximately 3 to 4 percent fat. Two percent or low-fat milk is half that.

Make your own preservative-free half-and-half by combining equal parts of milk and light cream. It is purer and fresher, but it won't last as long as commercially made half-and-half products that generally contain additives to lengthen the shelf life.

In years gone by, old-fashioned and homemade buttermilk were the by-products of making butter. Today, commercial buttermilk is produced by adding a bacterial culture to skim or fat-free or low-fat milk to create the texture and flavor of the original. Most labels indicate this with the words *cultured buttermilk*. It has a distinctively tart and tangy taste and should be used only in recipes where it's listed as an ingredient.

Most dairy products are marked with a "use by" date indicating their shelf life.

Yogurt

Yogurt is made from milk that is fermented by adding a bacteria or culture. It is then incubated until it is thick, creamy, and slightly acidic. Yogurt can be made from whole milk, low-fat, skim or fat-free milk, and all of these types are on the market.

Yogurt is usually packaged in containers ranging from eight ounces to one quart. My preference is low-fat. Fat-free yogurt has a thinner consistency than low-fat or whole milk versions and is not as pleasing to the palate in soup. Use plain yogurt, not a flavored one. Generally, yogurt lasts in the fridge for about one week after its expiration date.

Yogurt with active cultures has long been believed to be beneficial to health and to aid digestion.

Sour Cream

Sour cream is a cultured milk product with a thick, creamy texture and a delightfully tart taste, but unlike yogurt it has not been fermented. Instead, it has been chilled and aged for a day or two. Several types of sour cream are on the market, including whole milk, low-fat, and nonfat varieties, all of which are excellent choices for any recipe. They can be used interchangeably.

Tofu or Bean Curd

Found in the dairy case or produce section of many markets, tofu or bean curd is made from curdled soymilk that is pressed into a bar-shaped form. It is an excellent source of protein and calcium, low in calories, and cholesterol free. It has a satiny texture that is velvety smooth. The only drawback is its somewhat high sodium content. Tofu itself is bland and rather tasteless; however, it absorbs the flavor of the food to which it's added. It comes in firm and soft varieties, as well as silken varieties. If tofu is to be cubed for soup, it's best to use the firm variety that can be cubed easily and will not fall apart after it's added to simmering broth.

You'll sometimes find tofu sold in open tubs that are filled with water. To avoid any possible contamination, it's preferable to purchase tofu in a sealed container. Most tofu packages are dated. If not, keep the unopened package for 4 to 5 days after purchase. If you have some left over from a recipe, keep it for about 3 days submerged in a container of cold water, but remember to change the water daily. Always store fresh tofu in the refrigerator.

Tofu as a dairy substitute

Silken tofu is not pressed but coagulated and is sold in boxes. Puree it in a blender, and it will have a consistency similar to yogurt. It can be used in cream soups instead of cream or half-and-half, but must be stirred very well before adding. It won't alter any taste already in the soup.

Cheese

Cheeses are marvelously flavorful additions to creamy and pureed vegetable soups, as well as tasty garnishes for many heartier vegetable soups. These are used in the recipes in this book.

Cheddar

Whether domestic or imported from its native England, this highly popular, firm cheese can be purchased in a range of tastes from mild to sharp to very sharp, depending on how long it's aged. The longer it has been aged, the stronger its taste. After it's been opened, keep it in the refrigerator wrapped in plastic. To use it in soups, grate it on the largest side of a four-sided grater or in your food processor fitted with the shredding disk.

You should buy cheeses and grate them yourself for the freshest flavor, but that's not always possible when you're in a hurry. Some stores grate and package cheese on site. You can buy these in the dairy section of the supermarket. Figure 10-1 shows a cheese grater in action.

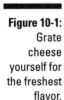

Figure 10-1:
Grate
cheese
yourself for
the freshest
flavor.

Parmesan and Romano

Both Parmesan and Romano, hard cheeses that have been aged for at least two and up to seven years, originally hail from Italy. Parmigiano Reggiano is Italy's superior Parmesan with a complex flavor and granular texture. Romano cheese comes in several varieties, one of the more famous being Pecorino Romano, which technically should be made from sheep's milk.

Buying domestic Parmesan or Romano for soups is fine, and several producers make good cheeses. For superior taste, try to buy wedges and grate the cheese yourself on a small-holed cheese grater or cut into pieces and pulse in a food processor fitted with the metal blade. Avoid canned or bottled Parmesan, which has little resemblance to the real thing. Store grated cheese in the refrigerator.

To keep cheese freshest, wrap wedges and slices in plastic and put grated cheese in an airtight container and refrigerate.

Blue

Blue cheese (also spelled "bleu"), with characteristic greenish-blue veins formed by mold, is known for its distinctively strong aroma and taste. Many countries have their own versions, although most styles are also made domestically. Examples of the more noted blues are French Roquefort, English Stilton, Italian Gorgonzola, Danish Danablu, and American Maytag. To use it in soups and salads, crumble it gently with your fingertips.

Swiss

A favorite among domestic cheeses, this firm, pale yellow cheese with large holes has a mildly nutty flavor. It imitates the popular imported Swiss Gruyere and Emmenthaler. Because Swiss cheese melts smoothly and doesn't become stringy, it is ideal for French Onion Soup. It can be thinly sliced or grated. Use the largest side of a four-sided grater or a food processor fitted with the shredding disk.

Cream Soups

Cream soups are the delightfully rich-tasting, velvety-textured soups that are no longer off limits to those worried about fat content. Lightened in response to modern dietary concerns, most of these soups are thickened with vegetable purees rather the traditional roux of butter and flour, and they are enriched with a minimum of milk, half-and-half, or cream. Two-percent or low-fat milk is acceptable, although the soup won't be as creamy, but skim or fat-free would make the soup too watery. Use whichever you prefer.

In most cases, if you divide the amount of cream or milk in the recipe by the number of portions, you'll find that each serving has only a tablespoon or two. If you prefer, omit the milk or cream and thin the soup with whatever broth or juice is used in the recipe, but keep in mind that dairy products are an excellent source of calcium. Follow the same rule when thinning a soup that's too thick.

Creamy Potato Leek Soup

Famous from France to Ireland, this filling soup, made of pureed potatoes and leeks, is a heavenly combination.

Yield: *6 servings*

Level: *Easy*

Tools: *Food processor, blender, or hand blender*

Preparation time: *15 minutes*

Cooking time: *45 minutes*

Freezes well

2 tablespoons butter

3 medium leeks, white part only, thinly sliced

1 medium onion, thinly sliced

4 cups chicken broth

1½ pounds potatoes, about 3 to 4 medium, peeled and thinly sliced

½ to ¾ cup cream, half-and-half, or milk

Salt to taste, about ½ teaspoon

¼ teaspoon black pepper

Chopped parsley for garnish

1 In a large pot over medium-low heat, melt the butter. Add the leeks and onions and sauté, stirring occasionally, until very tender and lightly golden, about 10 to 15 minutes.

2 Add the broth and potatoes. Increase the heat to medium and bring to a boil. Simmer, partially covered, until the potatoes are tender, about 25 to 30 minutes.

3 Puree in batches in a food processor or blender until smooth. Alternatively, if you have a hand blender, leave the soup in the pot and blend.

4 Return the soup to the pot. Thin it with cream. Add salt to taste and pepper. Heat thoroughly over medium heat. Serve garnished with chopped parsley.

Variation: *Make this soup with 1 pound of potatoes and ½ pound of carrots or parsnips, peeled and thinly sliced.*

Per Serving: *Calories 247.6; Protein 3.7g; Carbohydrates 28.1g; Dietary fiber 2.9g; Total fat 14.1g; Saturated fat 7.7g; Cholesterol 40.9mg; Sodium 882.1mg.*

Cream of Carrot Soup with Nutmeg

This inexpensive soup has a glorious orange color and spectacular taste.

Yield: *6 to 8 servings*

Level: *Easy*

Tools: *Food processor, blender, or hand blender*

Preparation time: *10 to 15 minutes*

Cooking time: *35 to 45 minutes*

Freezes well

1½ tablespoons butter or margarine

1 medium onion, chopped

4 cups chicken broth

1½ pounds carrots, peeled and coarsely chopped

½ bay leaf

¾ to 1 cup cream, half-and-half, or milk

¼ teaspoon freshly grated or ground nutmeg

Salt to taste, about ½ teaspoon

⅛ teaspoon white pepper

1½ tablespoons snipped fresh dill or chopped chives

1 In a large pot over medium heat, melt the butter. Add the onion, and sauté, stirring occasionally, until translucent, about 5 minutes.

2 Add the chicken broth, carrots, and bay leaf. Bring to a boil. Reduce the heat to medium-low. Cover and simmer until the carrots are tender, about 35 to 40 minutes.

3 Remove the bay leaf. Strain, reserving the broth. Puree the vegetables with some broth in batches in a food processor or blender. Alternatively, if you have a hand blender, leave the soup in the pot and blend.

4 In the same pot, combine the pureed vegetables, reserved broth, and half-and-half. Season with nutmeg, salt, and pepper. Reheat over medium heat, then stir in the dill.

Cook's Tip: *Carrots, a member of the parsley family, are an excellent source of the anti-oxidant beta-carotene, which the body turns into vitamin A. Beta-carotene is also found in broccoli.*

Per Serving: *Calories 155.6; Protein 2.0g; Carbohydrates 9.8g; Dietary fiber 2.8g; Total fat 12.6g; Saturated fat 7.0g; Cholesterol 38.9mg; Sodium 705.5mg.*

Creamy Carrot-Orange Soup

Fresh orange juice and zest add spark to the carrots in this simple soup. For a change, use fresh tangerine juice and its zest instead of orange.

Yield: *6 to 8 servings*

Level: *Easy*

Tools: *Food processor, blender, or hand blender*

Preparation time: *10 to 15 minutes*

Cooking time: *35 to 45 minutes*

Freezes well

1½ tablespoons butter or margarine	1½ teaspoons freshly grated orange zest
1 medium onion, chopped	¼ teaspoon freshly ground nutmeg
2½ cups chicken broth	Salt to taste, about ½ teaspoon
1½ cups fresh orange juice	⅛ to ¼ teaspoon cayenne
1½ pounds carrots, peeled and coarsely chopped	⅛ teaspoon white pepper
½ bay leaf	1½ teaspoons chopped fresh basil or chervil for garnish
¾ to 1 cup cream, half-and-half, or milk	1½ teaspoons chopped fresh chives or fresh chervil sprigs for garnish

1 In a large pot over medium heat, melt the butter. Add the onion and sauté, stirring occasionally, until translucent, about 5 minutes.

2 Add the chicken broth, orange juice, carrots, and bay leaf. Bring to a boil. Reduce the heat to medium-low. Cover and simmer until the carrots are tender, about 35 to 40 minutes.

3 Remove the bay leaf. Strain, reserving the broth. Puree the vegetables with some broth in batches in a food processor or blender. Alternatively, if you have a hand blender, leave the soup in the pot and blend.

4 In the same pot, combine the pureed vegetables, reserved broth, and half-and-half. Season with orange zest, nutmeg, salt, pepper, and cayenne. Reheat over medium heat. Garnish with herbs before serving.

Per Serving: *Calories 169.4; Protein 2.1g; Carbohydrates 14.7g; Dietary fiber 2.9g; Total fat 11.9g; Saturated fat 6.9g; Cholesterol 38.0mg; Sodium 518.7mg.*

Cream of Mushroom Soup

Not at all like its gloppy canned counterpart, this mushroom soup is light and has plenty of mushroom flavor.

Yield: *4 to 6 servings*

Level: *Easy*

Preparation time: *10 to 15 minutes*

Cooking time: *20 to 25 minutes*

Freezes well

2 tablespoons olive oil

2 tablespoons butter or margarine

1 medium onion, chopped

½ pound white or cremini mushrooms, coarsely chopped

3 tablespoons all-purpose flour

2½ cups mushroom, chicken, or beef broth

2 tablespoons dry sherry (optional)

⅓ to ½ cup half-and-half, cream, or milk

Salt to taste, about ½ teaspoon

Freshly ground black pepper to taste

1 tablespoon chopped fresh chives or parsley (optional)

1 In a medium saucepan over medium heat, heat the olive oil and butter. Add the onion and sauté, stirring occasionally, until translucent, about 5 minutes. Add the mushrooms and cook, stirring occasionally, for 5 minutes more.

2 Add the flour, and cook, stirring often, for 2 to 3 minutes.

3 Gradually pour in the broth, stirring after each addition. The soup should begin to thicken. Add the sherry (if desired).

4 Bring the soup to a boil. Cover partially and simmer over medium heat for 5 to 10 minutes. Add the cream and heat through. Season with salt and pepper. Stir in the chives.

Tip: *Use a combination of white, cremini, and shiitake (no shiitake stems) mushrooms for an earthier, richer taste.*

Per Serving: *Calories 134.6; Protein 2.0g; Carbohydrates 6.2g; Dietary fiber 1.0g; Total fat 11.7g; Saturated fat 4.4g; Cholesterol 17.3mg; Sodium 617.0mg.*

Tomato Orange Bisque

This unusual tomato soup is based on an old recipe from the Western Cape Province of South Africa. It's a knockout.

Yield: *4 to 6 servings*

Level: *Easy*

Tools: *Food processor, blender, or hand blender*

Preparation time: *15 minutes*

Cooking time: *50 to 60 minutes*

Freezes well

2 tablespoons olive oil

1 medium onion, chopped

1 carrot, chopped

1½ cups chicken broth

One 28-ounce can plum tomatoes with juice

½ cup fresh orange juice

1 bay leaf

½ teaspoon minced fresh thyme, or ¼ teaspoon dried thyme

1½ cups cream, half-and-half, or milk

2 teaspoons finely grated fresh orange zest

Salt to taste, about ½ to ¾ teaspoon

1 In a medium pot over medium heat, heat the olive oil. Add the onion and carrot and sauté, stirring occasionally, until translucent, about 5 minutes.

2 Add the broth, tomatoes, orange juice, bay leaf, and thyme. Simmer, partially covered, for 40 to 45 minutes.

3 With a slotted spoon, remove the bay leaf. Puree in batches in a food processor or blender until smooth. Alternatively, if you have a hand blender, leave the soup in the pot and blend.

4 Return the soup to the pot. Add the cream, orange zest, and salt and stir to blend. Reheat over medium heat, stirring occasionally.

Variation: *This soup is delightful cold, especially on a sweltering summer day. Chill the cooled soup in the refrigerator for 1 to 1½ hours.*

Per Serving: *Calories 301.0; Protein 3.2g; Carbohydrates 12.3g; Dietary fiber 2.0g; Total fat 27.8g; Saturated fat 14.6g; Cholesterol 82.8mg; Sodium 669.0mg.*

Clockwise from top: Carrot–Ginger Soup (Chapter 15);
Curried Zucchini Soup (Chapter 9); Herbed Beet Soup (Chapter 9)

South-of-the-Border Black Bean Soup (Chapter 8)

Spicy Pumpkin and Corn Chowder (Chapter 9)

Nana's Beef, Vegetable, and Barley Soup (Chapter 11)

From top: Italian Chicken, Greens, and Tortellini Soup; Spanish Garlic Soup with Cheese Dumplings (both in Chapter 14)

From top: Indonesian Shrimp Soup with Noodles; Mulligatawny Soup (both in Chapter 14)

Curried Mussel Soup (Chapter 14)

Cantaloupe–Orange Soup;
Very Berry Fruit Gazpacho
(both in Chapter 15)

Cream of Tomato Soup Variations

I always think of this soup as comfort food. Here are two healthful ways to prepare it.

Yield: 4 to 6 servings

Level: Easy

Tools: Food processor, blender, or hand blender

Preparation time: 15 minutes

Cooking time: 50 to 60 minutes

Freezes well

Variation 1

1 Prepare the Creamy Tomato Orange Bisque earlier in this chapter.

2 Substitute an additional ½ cup chicken broth for the orange juice.

3 Add 2 to 4 teaspoons sugar when adding the tomatoes and broth. Omit the grated fresh orange zest.

4 Garnish with homemade croutons.

Variation 2

1 Prepare the Fresh Tomato Basil Soup in Chapter 9.

2 After pureeing the ingredients, add ½ to ⅔ cup cream, half-and-half, or milk and reheat. Omit the basil or pesto if you want.

Cook's Fact: Andy Warhol created his renowned pop art serigraph of the Campbell's Tomato Soup can in 1965.

Measuring up

Measuring butter and margarine out of a tub can be tricky. Use butter or margarine in sticks instead of out of a tub, because it's much easier to measure. Here's a handy guide:

✔ ¼ pound = 1 stick

✔ 1 stick = ½ cup or 8 tablespoons

✔ ½ stick = 4 tablespoons

✔ ¼ stick = 2 tablespoons

✔ ⅛ stick = 1 tablespoon

Easy Creamy Spinach Soup

This lovely soup, thickened with rice, is a snap to make and always delicious.

Yield: *6 servings*

Level: *Easy*

Tools: *Food processor, blender, or hand blender*

Preparation time: *5 to 10 minutes*

Cooking time: *30 to 35 minutes*

Freezes well

2 tablespoons vegetable oil	½ teaspoon freshly ground black pepper
1 medium onion, chopped	⅛ teaspoon ground nutmeg
3½ cups chicken broth	Salt to taste, about ½ teaspoon
¼ cup white rice	½ to ¾ cup half-and-half, cream, or milk
One 10-ounce package frozen, chopped spinach	

1 In a large pot over medium heat, heat the vegetable oil. Add the onion and sauté, stirring occasionally, until translucent, about 5 minutes.

2 Add the chicken broth and rice. Cover and bring to a boil. Reduce the heat to medium-low and simmer, partially covered, until the rice is tender, about 15 to 20 minutes.

3 Add the spinach, pepper, and nutmeg. Simmer until the spinach is cooked, about 10 minutes.

4 Puree in batches in a food processor or blender until smooth. Alternatively, if you have a hand blender, leave the soup in the pot and blend.

5 Return the soup to the pot and season with salt. Reduce the heat to medium-low, add the cream, and heat thoroughly.

Tip: This is a good soup to make when unexpected guests stay for lunch or supper because you're likely to have the ingredients on hand.

Per Serving: Calories 135.0; Protein 3.0g; Carbohydrates 10.5g; Dietary fiber 1.3g; Total fat 9.4g; Saturated fat 2.4g; Cholesterol 10.4mg; Sodium 812.3mg.

Cream of Asparagus Soup

This delicate soup is a real spring treat and should be made with fresh asparagus, which is available from February through June. When it is out of season, imports are available, but they can be costly.

Yield: *4 to 6 servings*

Level: *Easy*

Tools: *Food processor, blender, or hand blender*

Preparation time: *10 minutes*

Cooking time: *20 to 25 minutes*

Freezes well

1 pound asparagus, washed and trimmed

2 tablespoons butter or margarine

1 medium onion, chopped

⅓ cup dry white wine or vermouth (optional)

3 cups chicken broth

1 cup cream or half-and-half

Salt to taste, about ½ teaspoon

⅛ teaspoon white pepper

Freshly grated Romano cheese for garnish (optional)

1 Slice off the asparagus tips at an angle and reserve, about 1 cup. Coarsely chop the stalks. Set aside.

2 In a large pot over medium heat, melt the butter. Add the onion, and sauté, stirring occasionally, until tender, about 10 minutes. Add the white wine (if desired) and cook for 1 to 2 minutes.

3 Add the chicken broth. Cover and bring to a boil. Add the chopped stalks, and cook, covered, until the stalks are very tender, about 10 to 12 minutes.

4 Puree in batches in a food processor or blender until smooth. Alternatively, if you have a hand blender, leave the soup in the pot and blend.

5 Return the soup to the pot. Add the cream and reserved asparagus tips. Season with salt and pepper and simmer over medium heat until the tips are tender-crisp. Serve with freshly grated Romano cheese on the side.

Tip: *Instead of using the whole spear, reserve the tender tips for a side dish and make the soup with only the 1 pound of trimmed stalks.*

Per Serving: *Calories 135.0; Protein 3.0g; Carbohydrates 10.5g; Dietary fiber 1.3g; Total fat 9.4g; Saturated fat 2.4g; Cholesterol 10.4mg; Sodium 812.3mg.*

Cream of Cauliflower Soup

Being a cauliflower lover, I think this is the ultimate cream soup. It's marvelous either with cream or milk, or without, if thinned with additional broth.

Yield: *6 to 8 servings*

Level: *Easy*

Tools: *Food processor, blender, or hand blender*

Preparation time: *10 minutes*

Cooking time: *40 to 45 minutes*

Freezes well

2 tablespoons butter or margarine

1 small onion, chopped

½ cup dry white wine or vermouth (optional)

4½ cups chicken or vegetable broth

1¼ pounds cauliflower, coarsely chopped, about 6 cups

1 cup cream, half-and-half, or milk

Salt to taste, about ½ to ¾ teaspoon

⅛ teaspoon white pepper

1 In a large pot over medium heat, melt the butter. Add the onion and cook, stirring occasionally, until translucent, about 5 minutes.

2 Add the wine (if desired) and cook for 2 minutes. Add the broth and cauliflower. Cover and simmer until the cauliflower is very tender, about 30 to 35 minutes.

3 Puree in batches in a food processor or blender until smooth. Alternatively, if you have a hand blender, leave the soup in the pot and blend.

4 Return the soup to the pot and add the cream. Season with salt and pepper, and reheat over medium heat.

Cook's Fact: *Broccoflower, the offspring of the cauliflower and broccoli, has a milder flavor and would be suitable for any of the soups that feature either of its parents.*

Per Serving: *Calories 168.3; Protein 2.5g; Carbohydrates 4.1g; Dietary fiber 2.0g; Total fat 16.5g; Saturated fat 9.3g; Cholesterol 51.4mg; Sodium 729.3mg.*

Cream of Broccoli Soup

If you're a broccoli fan, this easy soup will hit the spot. If you like, you can prepare the soup with only chopped stems (about 6 cups) and reserve the florets for another use.

Yield: *6 to 8 servings*

Level: *Easy*

Tools: *Food processor, blender, or hand blender*

Preparation time: *10 minutes*

Cooking time: *45 to 50 minutes*

Freezes well

2 tablespoons butter or margarine

1 small onion, chopped

5 cups chicken or vegetable broth

1¼ pounds broccoli, coarsely chopped, about 6 cups

1 cup cream, half-and-half, or milk

Salt to taste, about ½ to ¾ teaspoon

¼ teaspoon freshly ground black pepper

1 In a large pot over medium heat, melt the butter. Add the onion and cook, stirring occasionally, until translucent, about 5 minutes.

2 Add the broth and broccoli. Cover and simmer until the broccoli is very tender, about 25 to 30 minutes.

3 Puree in batches in a food processor or blender until smooth. Alternatively, if you have a hand blender, leave the soup in the pot and blend.

4 Return the soup to the pot and add the cream. Season with salt and pepper and reheat over medium heat.

Cook's Fact: *A nutritional superstar, broccoli is an excellent source of vitamins A and C, as well as calcium, iron, and fiber.*

Per Serving: *Calories 168.3; Protein 2.5g; Carbohydrates 4.1g; Dietary fiber 2.0g; Total fat 16.5g; Saturated fat 9.3g; Cholesterol 51.4mg; Sodium 729.3mg.*

Broccoli Cheddar Soup

Not much can top the superb duo of broccoli and cheese. This soup has a luxuriously rich texture and taste.

Yield: *6 to 8 servings*

Level: *Easy*

Tools: *Food processor, blender, or hand blender*

Preparation time: *10 minutes*

Cooking time: *45 to 50 minutes*

Do not freeze

2 tablespoons butter or margarine	*½ cup cream, half-and-half, or milk*
1 medium onion, chopped	*6 ounces grated Cheddar cheese*
4 cups chicken or vegetable broth	*Salt to taste, about ¼ to ½ teaspoon*
1 pound broccoli, coarsely chopped, about 4 to 5 cups	*Freshly ground black pepper to taste*

1 In a large pot over medium heat, melt the butter. Add the onion and sauté, stirring occasionally, until translucent, about 5 minutes.

2 Add the broth and broccoli. Cover and simmer until the broccoli is very tender, about 35 to 40 minutes.

3 Puree in batches in a food processor or blender until smooth. Alternatively, if you have a hand blender, leave the soup in the pot and blend.

4 Return the soup to the pot over medium heat, add the cream and cheese, and stir until the cheese is melted. Season with salt and pepper.

Cook's Fact: *White Cheddar is naturally white; yellow Cheddar is colored with annatto, a natural dye.*

Tip: *Use medium, sharp, or extra sharp Cheddar, whichever you prefer, in the soups.*

Per Serving: *Calories 201.1; Protein 7.8g; Carbohydrates 4.3g; Dietary fiber 1.7g; Total fat 17.6g; Saturated fat 10.2g; Cholesterol 53.0mg; Sodium 724.3mg.*

Creamy Cheddar Cheese Soup

Red bell pepper and cheddar cheese give this soup, thickened with potatoes, an outstanding taste. It's too filling to be served as anything other than the main course. If you like it hotter, add extra cayenne or serve with Tabasco on the side.

Yield: *6 to 8 servings*

Level: *Easy*

Tools: *Food processor, blender, or hand blender*

Preparation time: *15 minutes*

Cooking time: *35 to 40 minutes*

Do not freeze

2 tablespoons vegetable oil

2 medium onions, chopped

1 small or medium red bell pepper, peeled and diced

3½ cups chicken or vegetable broth

2 medium potatoes, about 12 ounces, peeled and diced

½ to ¾ cup milk

8 ounces coarsely grated Cheddar cheese, about 2¼ cups

Salt to taste, about ¼ to ½ teaspoon

¼ teaspoon freshly ground black pepper

⅛ to ¼ teaspoon cayenne (optional)

Homemade bacon bits or croutons for garnish (optional)

1 In a large pot over medium heat, heat the vegetable oil. Add the onions and bell pepper and sauté, stirring occasionally until the onions are lightly golden, about 10 to 15 minutes.

2 Add the chicken broth and potatoes. Cover and simmer until the potatoes are tender, about 25 to 30 minutes.

3 Puree in batches in a food processor or blender until smooth. Alternatively, if you have a hand blender, leave the soup in the pot and blend.

4 Return the soup to the pot, and reduce the heat to medium-low. Add the milk and cheese and stir until the cheese is melted. Thin with additional milk or broth if it's too thick. Season with salt, pepper, and cayenne (if desired). Garnish with bacon bits or croutons.

Tip: *To peel the bell pepper easily, slice off the top and bottom ends and cut the pepper in half. Peel with a vegetable peeler. You can also substitute a small roasted red bell pepper.*

Per Serving: Calories 213.7; Protein 9.0g; Carbohydrates 11.0g; Dietary fiber 1.2g; Total fat 15.2g; Saturated fat 7.0g; Cholesterol 34.0mg; Sodium 695.8mg.

Chapter 11

Soup from the Butcher

Meat and poultry are the mainstay of a multitude of dishes including soups, adding their individual character and depth of flavor. These versatile ingredients, the basis of delicious broth, act as the predominate component in several hearty soups, as well as agreeable accents in lighter fare.

As with any fresh food item, the quality of the ingredients affects the quality of the finished dish. Always purchase meat and poultry from a reputable store — a good supermarket or butcher. When buying prepacked items, check the sell-by date on the label. It's best to use it by that day or freeze it. Often, you'll find that today's bargain or what's on sale must be used right away or frozen. If you decide to freeze meat or poultry, take it out of the store's packaging. Never just toss it in the freezer. Rewrap the item in plastic wrap, and then in foil or freezer wrap, or use a self-sealing plastic bag to protect it from freezer-burn. Label and date it so you know how long it's been in your freezer, and use it within two months.

Meat

Cooks used to make their own beef stock using bones, but now bones are not always available in supermarkets. The recipes in this book call for broth such as the Beef Broth that you'll find in Chapter 5, which can be made with only meat or the canned variety. If you do find bones, you can try making Browned Beef Broth, also in Chapter 5.

The meat used in soups is generally the same cut that is used in stews, because both dishes tend to simmer slowly for an hour or two until the meat is tender. Meat should be well marbled and yes, that means you should see some strands of fat running through the meat. Otherwise, the meat will become tough and stringy. Trim visible excess fat from the outer edges. Whether you're making a beef or lamb soup, pass up packages labeled "stew or soup meat." Often, they're low quality and include scraps that can be quite fatty. Instead, look for a specific cut that is cubed or buy a whole piece of meat and cube it yourself.

Look for the following cuts of meat when you want to prepare soup:

- **Beef:** Chuck, shin, or bottom round, cubed, or leaner top round, cubed, are excellent for soup. If you don't mind bones, short ribs cut into 3-inch pieces are also a good choice.
- **Oxtail:** Cut into pieces between the joints, oxtail can be used for broth or soup. It can be fatty, so you might want to chill it and remove the fat once it has solidified as directed in Chapter 4.
- **Lamb:** Shoulder, cubed, is good for soup and broth.

When handling fresh meat and poultry, hygiene is important. To prevent bacterial contamination, wash cutting boards and utensils in hot, soapy water after use and rinse well. And don't forget to wash countertops and hands as well.

Poultry

Years ago, stewing hens, also called fowl, were readily available. These tougher birds made wonderful broths, soups, and stews, but now they're very hard to find. Sometimes, you may want to make your own broth but not use the meat; other times, you'll make the stock and want to add the meat to a soup later. Still other times, you'll simply add the meat to premade broth, such as the Chicken Broth or Browned Chicken Broth recipes in Chapter 5, or canned chicken broth.

Remember to wash whole chickens or turkey and chicken or turkey parts with cold water and pat dry with a paper towel before using. If bits of the innards or blood are left on the poultry, scrub the meat gently with coarse or kosher salt and rinse well.

To minimize any potential health hazards, defrost poultry and meat overnight in the refrigerator.

Use this list to determine what cuts of poultry to buy for the types of soups you're making:

- ✔ **Best for broth only:** Chicken or turkey parts such as thighs, legs, backs, necks, and wings, or a meaty turkey carcass, cut up, make the tastiest broth.
- ✔ **Best for broth when meat is also added to finished soup:** A whole chicken, which has been cut up or more richly flavored dark meat parts, such as thighs or legs from chicken or turkey, are good choices.
- ✔ **Poultry meat to add to soup:** Boneless chicken breasts or thighs; meat from turkey thighs; leftover chicken; and leftover turkey breast or thighs can be cooked or used raw. Cube or cut into strips as the recipe indicates.

Remember that you can always substitute turkey whenever chicken is called for in the recipes in this book.

Hearty Meat and Poultry Soups

Fortifying and robust, meat and poultry soups are especially enjoyable when the air gets cooler. They are substantial enough to be considered a main course, requiring only bread or crackers and perhaps a salad on the side. In winter, I like to keep them on hand in the freezer. Most chicken soups can be made in a relatively short amount of time; however, the meat soups must simmer for an hour or two so that the meat becomes very tender.

Half or whole?

Did you ever wonder why ½ a bay leaf is called for? Too much of it will make a dish taste bitter. There are two types of bay leaves. The Turkish variety has smaller leaves and a milder flavor than the California laurel, the kind that's mainly sold in the United States. If you come across fresh bay leaves, use them sparingly because they're much more pungent than dried.

Nana's Beef, Vegetable, and Barley Soup

Warming and wonderful, this winter soup is a freezer favorite in my house. Add more broth if the soup or leftovers become too thick. You can replace the frozen vegetables with fresh if you want. You can also substitute peas for the lima beans or string beans, but add them only at the time you would add the string beans.

Yield: *12 to 14 servings*

Level: *Easy*

Preparation time: *15 to 20 minutes*

Cooking time: *1½ to 1¾ hours*

Freezes well

One 28-ounce can whole plum tomatoes with juice, broken into pieces with the back of a wooden spoon

8 to 10 cups beef broth or water

1 pound beef chuck, shin, or bottom round, cut into 1-inch cubes or 1½ to 2 pounds short ribs, cut into pieces

1 medium to large onion, quartered and thinly sliced

2 medium carrots, sliced

2 celery stalks, sliced

One 10-ounce package frozen corn kernels

One 10-ounce package frozen lima beans

1½ cups shredded Savoy or green cabbage

⅓ cup pearl barley

1 bay leaf

One 10-ounce package frozen string beans

Salt to taste, about ½ to 1 teaspoon

Freshly ground black pepper to taste

1 In a large pot over medium heat, combine the tomatoes, 8 cups of broth, beef, onion, carrots, celery, corn, lima beans, cabbage, barley, and bay leaf. Cover and bring to a boil.

2 Reduce the heat to medium-low. Simmer, partially covered, until the meat, barley, and vegetables are tender, about 1½ hours. Using a ladle or skimmer, remove any foam that forms during the cooking time and add additional broth if too much liquid has evaporated.

3 Add the string beans and stir. Thin, if necessary, with additional broth or water. Simmer for 15 to 20 minutes. Season with salt and freshly ground black pepper.

Per Serving: *Calories 170.1; Protein 12.2g; Carbohydrates 18.4g; Dietary fiber 4.4g; Total fat 5.7g; Saturated fat 2.2g; Cholesterol 22.1mg; Sodium 775.3mg.*

Spanky's Beef Soup with Tomatoes and Potatoes

Economical and filling, this tasty beef soup is one of the easiest recipes.

Yield: *6 to 8 servings*

Level: *Easy*

Preparation time: *15 minutes*

Cooking time: *1¼ to 1½ hours*

Freezes well

One 14-ounce can whole tomatoes with juice, broken into pieces with the back of a wooden spoon

4 cups beef broth or water

1 pound beef chuck, shin, or bottom round, cut into 1-inch cubes

1 medium onion, quartered and thinly sliced

2 medium potatoes, about 12 ounces, peeled and diced

2 celery stalks, sliced

1 carrot, sliced

2 plump cloves garlic, peeled and coarsely chopped

½ bay leaf

1 teaspoon fresh thyme leaves, about 1 sprig, or ½ teaspoon dried thyme

Salt to taste

Freshly ground black pepper to taste

2 tablespoons chopped fresh flat-leaf parsley

1 In a large pot over medium heat, combine the tomatoes, broth, beef, onion, potatoes, celery, carrot, garlic, bay leaf, and thyme.

2 Reduce the heat to medium-low. Simmer, partially covered, until the meat and vegetables are tender, about 1¼ to 1½ hours. Skim off any foam that forms during the cooking process.

3 Remove the bay leaf. Season with salt and pepper and stir in the parsley.

Per Serving: *Calories 192.9; Protein 14.2g; Carbohydrates 12.3g; Dietary fiber 1.8g; Total fat 9.4g; Saturated fat 3.7g; Cholesterol 38.7mg; Sodium 689.4mg.*

Herbed Oxtail and Vegetable Soup

Oxtail makes an exquisitely rich and flavorful broth. Although this soup takes time, it's well worth the wait.

Because oxtail soup can be fatty, you might want to make it the day before serving it. Cool and refrigerate it according to the instructions in Chapter 4. You can then easily remove the excess fat that has risen to the surface of the cold soup. Reheat it to serve.

Yield: *8 to 10 servings*

Level: *Easy*

Preparation time: *15 to 20 minutes*

Cooking time: *3 to 3½ hours*

Freezes well

2 pounds oxtail, cut into sections between the joints

½ teaspoon salt

¼ teaspoon freshly ground black pepper

1½ tablespoons olive oil

1 medium onion, chopped

2 carrots, chopped

2 celery stalks, chopped

2 plump cloves garlic, chopped

5¼ cups water

One 14-ounce can tomatoes with juice, broken with the back of a wooden spoon, or 2 to 3 medium tomatoes, peeled, seeded, and chopped

¾ cup hearty red wine or additional water

1 bay leaf

1 teaspoon fresh thyme leaves, or ½ teaspoon dried thyme

½ teaspoon fresh chopped rosemary, or ½ teaspoon dried and crumbled rosemary

2 tablespoons chopped fresh flat-leaf parsley

Additional salt to taste, about ½ to 1 teaspoon

Additional freshly ground black pepper

1 Season the oxtail with salt and pepper. In a large pot over medium heat, heat the olive oil. Add the oxtail and lightly brown each piece on all sides.

2 Add the onion, carrots, and celery and sauté, stirring occasionally, for 3 to 4 minutes. Add the garlic and cook, stirring often, for 1 minute.

3 Add the water, tomatoes, wine, bay leaf, thyme, and rosemary. Cover and bring to a boil.

4 Reduce the heat to medium-low and simmer, partially covered, until the meat is very tender, about 3 to 3½ hours. Skim off any foam and ladle off visible surface fat as necessary. Add 1 to 2 cups additional water as the liquid evaporates.

5 Stir in the parsley and season with salt and freshly ground black pepper.

Cook's Fact: *Oxtail actually comes from a beef or veal tail and requires slow cooking to become tender. It is normally sold disjointed, but if not, have the butcher cut it into pieces between the joints.*

Per Serving: Calories 298.4; Protein 29.6g; Carbohydrates 13.6g; Dietary fiber 2.2g; Total fat 14.1g; Saturated fat 5.1g; Cholesterol 93.6mg; Sodium 905.3mg.

Scotch Broth

Centuries old, this renowned Scottish soup is always made with lamb or mutton and barley. You may have to search for lamb bones — ask your butcher. If you can't find them, leave them out.

Yield: *10 to 12 servings*

Level: *Easy*

Preparation time: *15 minutes*

Cooking time: *1¾ to 2 hours*

Freezes well

1¼ to 1½ pounds lean lamb from shoulder, trimmed and cut into ¾-inch cubes

1 pound lamb bones (optional)

8 cups water

½ cup pearl barley

1 medium onion, chopped

1 celery stalk, finely diced

1 medium carrot, finely diced

Salt to taste, about ½ to 1 teaspoon

½ teaspoon freshly ground black pepper

2 tablespoons chopped fresh parsley

1 In a large pot over medium heat, combine the lamb, lamb bones (if desired), and water. Cover and bring to a boil. Reduce the heat to medium-low. Simmer, partially covered, for 45 to 55 minutes, skimming off any foam or fat occasionally. With a slotted spoon, remove the bones.

2 Add the barley, onion, celery, and carrot. Simmer, partially covered, until the barley and vegetables are tender, about 50 to 60 minutes. Add more broth or water if necessary.

3 Season with salt and pepper and stir in the parsley.

Tip: *For a more robust flavor, make the broth with part water and part beef or chicken broth.*

Per Serving: Calories 106.9; Protein 10.9g; Carbohydrates 8.0g; Dietary fiber 1.7g; Total fat 3.3g; Saturated fat 1.2g; Cholesterol 32.6mg; Sodium 139.5mg.

Old-Fashioned Chicken or Turkey Rice Soup

This simple recipe features the true, from-scratch method of making chicken or turkey soup. Vary it by adding a few cooked or frozen vegetables in the last step.

The process used in this recipe is the conventional way to start many chicken based soups. In most recipes, however, I use chicken broth and chicken (raw or cooked, and chopped or shredded as directed), which saves a lot of time for a busy cook. If you have the time or the inclination, you can, of course, choose to begin other soups by following the old-fashioned method in Steps 1 through 5 of this recipe.

Using a cut-up meaty, leftover carcass from a roasted chicken or turkey instead of raw chicken parts works and is economical, but you may need to reinforce the broth by adding a few raw chicken or turkey parts or leftover meat; otherwise, the broth may taste too watery and weak.

Yield: *6 servings*

Level: *Easy*

Preparation time: *10 minutes*

Cooking time: *1½ to 2 hours*

Freezes well

1½ tablespoons vegetable oil	½ bay leaf
1 carrot, chopped	6 to 7 cups water
1 celery stalk, chopped	½ cup white rice
1 small onion, chopped	Salt to taste, about ¾ to 1 teaspoon
2 to 2½ pounds chicken parts, preferably backs, thighs, legs, and wings	Freshly ground black pepper to taste
	Chopped fresh parsley for garnish

1 In a large pot over medium heat, heat the vegetable oil. Add the carrot, celery, and onion and sauté, stirring occasionally, until the onion is translucent, about 5 minutes.

2 Add the chicken or turkey parts and bay leaf and cover with the water. Use additional water, if necessary, making sure that the chicken is covered totally with water.

3 Cover partiallyand bring to a gentle boil. Skim off any foam.

4 Reduce the heat to medium-low and simmer, partially covered, until the poultry is tender, about 1½ to 2 hours. Skim off any foam and fat as they form. Add more water if too much has evaporated.

5 Strain the solids from the broth and discard the vegetables and bay leaf. Remove the meat from the chicken and reserve it, but discard the skin and bone. Skim off any fat or chill as directed in Chapter 4 before continuing to help remove the fat. Shred or cut the meat into bite-size pieces.

6 Return the broth to a gentle boil. Add the rice and the reserved meat and simmer, uncovered, until the rice is tender, about 15 to 20 minutes. Season with salt and pepper and garnish with parsley.

Per Serving: Calories 272.5; Protein 22.7g; Carbohydrates 13.4g; Dietary fiber 0.2g; Total fat 13.4g; Saturated fat 3.0g; Cholesterol 72.9mg; Sodium 361.0mg.

Chicken and Corn Soup

Hale and hardy, this traditional American soup comes from the farm kitchens of the Pennsylvania Dutch.

Hard-boiled eggs do not freeze well, so if you want to make a batch of this soup and freeze any leftovers, add the chopped, hard-boiled eggs to individual serving bowls, not to the pot. Then leftovers can be frozen without the eggs.

Yield: *6 to 8 servings*

Level: *Easy*

Preparation time: *10 minutes*

Cooking time: *25 minutes*

Do not freeze

5½ cups chicken broth

½ pound boneless chicken breasts, cut into bite-size pieces, or 1 cup cooked, cubed chicken

1¼ cups fresh corn kernels, or one 10-ounce package frozen corn kernels

2 ounces fine egg noodles, about 1¼ cups

Salt to taste, about ½ to ¾ teaspoon

¼ teaspoon freshly ground black pepper

1 to 2 hard-boiled eggs, chopped

1 tablespoon chopped fresh parsley

1 In a large pot over medium heat, combine the broth, chicken, and corn. Cover partially and simmer or until the chicken is cooked, about 15 minutes.

2 Add the noodles and cook until the noodles are tender, about 8 to 10 minutes. Season with salt and pepper.

3 Remove from the heat. Add the hard-boiled eggs and parsley.

Per Serving: Calories 124.8; Protein 9.8g; Carbohydrates 11.5g; Dietary fiber 1.4g; Total fat 4.7g; Saturated fat 1.1g; Cholesterol 52.5mg; Sodium 855mg.

Country Chicken Noodle Soup

Nothing beats this chunky chicken noodle soup on a cool day.

Yield: *6 to 8 servings*

Level: *Easy*

Preparation time: *10 minutes*

Cooking time: *25 to 30 minutes*

Freezes well

2 tablespoons vegetable oil

1 small onion, quartered and thinly sliced

1 small celery stalk, finely diced

1 small carrot, finely diced

5½ cups chicken broth

4 ounces boneless chicken, diced, or ½ cup diced, cooked chicken

½ teaspoon minced fresh thyme leaves, or ¼ teaspoon dried thyme

1½ to 1¾ cups short, broad egg noodles, about 3½ ounces

1¼ cups fresh peas or string beans, or one 10-ounce package frozen peas or string beans

Salt to taste, about ½ to ¾ teaspoon

¼ teaspoon freshly ground black pepper

1½ tablespoons chopped fresh parsley

1 In a large pot over medium heat, heat the vegetable oil. Add the onion, celery, and carrot and sauté, stirring occasionally, until softened, about 10 to 15 minutes.

2 Add the broth, chicken, and thyme. Cover and simmer until the chicken is cooked and the vegetables are very tender, about 15 minutes.

3 Add the noodles and peas. Simmer, uncovered, until the noodles are tender, about 10 to 12 minutes. Season with salt and pepper. Stir in the parsley.

Per Serving: *Calories 123.1; Protein 6.2g; Carbohydrates 9.3g; Dietary fiber 1.1g; Total fat 6.8g; Saturated fat 1.1g; Cholesterol 17.6mg; Sodium 853.2mg.*

Easy Chicken or Turkey Vegetable Soup

Ever popular, chicken (and turkey) soup has many variations. This is another effortless way to make it.

Give this soup an Italian flair by stirring in a tablespoon or two of fresh chopped basil or basil pesto. Serve it with freshly grated Parmesan or Romano cheese.

Yield: 6 to 8 servings

Level: Easy

Preparation time: 15 to 20 minutes

Cooking time: 35 to 40 minutes

Freezes well

2 tablespoons vegetable or olive oil

1 medium onion, quartered and thinly sliced

1 medium carrot, diced

1 celery stalk, diced (1 tablespoon of leaves chopped and reserved)

1 plump clove garlic, minced (optional)

6 cups chicken or turkey broth

2 cups vegetables (choose from root veggies and other veggies)

1 to 1½ cups cooked and cubed or shredded chicken or turkey

Salt to taste, about ½ to ¾ teaspoon

Freshly ground black pepper to taste

2 tablespoons minced fresh parsley

Root veggies

½ cup chopped turnip or rutabaga

½ cup diced peeled potato

½ cup diced sweet potato

Other veggies

½ cup fresh or frozen corn kernels

½ cup fresh or frozen peas

½ cup fresh or frozen string beans

½ cup chopped green or Savoy cabbage

½ cup diced zucchini

½ cup diced yellow squash

½ drained, canned tomatoes, chopped or stewed

1 In a large pot over medium heat, heat the vegetable oil. Add the onion, carrot, and celery, and sauté, stirring occasionally, until softened, about 10 minutes. Add the garlic and cook, stirring, for 1 minute.

2 Add the broth and any selections from the root veggies list. Cover and bring to a gentle boil. Then cover partially and simmer until the vegetables are almost tender, about 10 to 15 minutes.

3 Add your choices from the other veggies list. Add more broth if you want to add more veggies than suggested or if the soup is too chunky for you. Add the chicken and stir. Simmer, uncovered, until the vegetables are tender, about 10 to 12 minutes.

4 Season with salt and pepper. Stir in the parsley and reserved celery leaves.

Per Serving: Calories 273.8; Protein 22.3g; Carbohydrates 7.1g; Dietary fiber 1.4g; Total fat 17.0g; Saturated fat 3.9g; Cholesterol 68.9mg; Sodium 965.1mg.

Chicken and Sausage Gumbo

Straight from Cajun country to your table, this gumbo is fantastic. Make sure that all ingredients are prepped and ready before you begin making the roux, which is the only tricky step in preparing this soup.

Yield: *6 to 8 servings*

Level: *Intermediate to challenging*

Preparation time: *20 minutes*

Cooking time: *2 to 2½ hours*

Freezes well

For the roux

⅓ cup vegetable oil

⅓ cup all-purpose flour

For the gumbo

1 medium onion, chopped, about ½ cup

5 scallions, white part only, sliced, about ¼ cup

1 celery stalk, chopped, about ½ cup

1 small to medium green bell pepper, chopped, about ½ cup

6 cups chicken broth, heated

1 pound boneless, skinless chicken breasts or thighs, cut into thin, bite-size strips

¼ to ⅓ pound andouille or chorizo sausage, sliced

1 to 1½ teaspoons cayenne or to taste

½ teaspoon ground black pepper

¼ teaspoon ground white pepper

½ teaspoon minced fresh thyme leaves, or ¼ teaspoon dried thyme

Salt to taste, about ½ to ¾ teaspoon

1 tablespoon gumbo filé (optional)

2 tablespoons chopped fresh parsley

1½ cups cooked rice

Tabasco sauce

1 **To make the roux:** In a heavy Dutch oven or deep skillet (preferably cast iron or enameled cast iron) over low heat, combine the oil and flour. Cook, stirring frequently, pushing the mixture off the bottom and stirring in a circular motion, until the roux becomes a rich, golden brown color. This process can take up to 45 minutes to 1 hour, but be careful not to burn the roux. It should be brown, but not blackened.

2 **To make the gumbo:** Add the onion, scallions, celery, and bell pepper to the roux and increase the temperature to medium-low. Cook, stirring almost constantly until the vegetables are softened, about 7 to 10 minutes.

3 Gradually ladle in the warmed chicken broth, stirring after each addition. Bring the mixture to a boil and continue stirring.

4 Add the chicken, sausage, 1 teaspoon of cayenne, black pepper, white pepper, and thyme. Cover partially (or it will boil over and make a mess) and simmer for 45 to 60 minutes. Skim the surface with a ladle to remove any fat that rises.

5 Taste for salt and season as necessary. You may want to add more cayenne. Add the gumbo filé (if desired) and parsley and stir to blend. Serve in soup bowls over rice with Tabasco sauce on the side.

Cook's Fact: *Gumbo filé or filé powder is made from ground sassafras leaves and has an earthy flavor. Used in Cajun cooking, it is available in the spice section of supermarkets and specialty markets.*

Per Serving: *Calories 268.9; Protein 17.7g; Carbohydrates 6.5g; Dietary fiber 0.8g; Total fat 18.9g; Saturated fat 3.8g; Cholesterol 49.8mg; Sodium 1105.0mg.*

The secret of making a roux

Never rush a roux! A good roux, a combination of vegetable oil and flour, takes plenty of time and should be cooked slowly over low heat. Remember to heat the chicken broth to a gentle simmer. Do not add cold chicken broth or the roux will turn lumpy. If any dark brown or black specks are in the roux, it has burned and must be thrown away. You'll need to start from scratch in a clean pot.

Chapter 12

Soup from the Fishmonger

In This Chapter

▶ Buying and preparing fresh or frozen seafood

▶ Creating fish and shellfish chowder and bisque recipes

Seafood is not only for main courses! Those who live along the coast or near lakes and rivers have made fish and shellfish the star of many beloved soups and traditional chowders. I've listed a few ethnic soups from other chapters in the recipe list so that you'll find them easily if you want a more exotic-tasting seafood soup.

When selecting seafood, buy the best quality fish or shellfish that you can from a reliable market that keeps fish on ice or in a refrigerated case. Fishmongers with high turnover often have the freshest product, which directly translates into the best-tasting soup. Poor seafood can ruin any dish. Neither the market nor the seafood should have an offensively strong smell. Because large fisheries now flash-freeze products, they're often preferable to fresh that is of questionable quality.

Buying Fish

Fresh fish fillets and scallops should be firm to the touch and have no bruises or brown spots that might indicate spoilage. Whole fish should have gills that are moist and red or bright pink, eyes that are clear and bulging (not milky or sunken), and bright, shiny scales. Frozen products should have no signs of freezer burn, such as excessive ice crystals, dried out, or chalky looking. The shells of clams and mussels should be closed. Shrimp should not have yellowed or blackened shells. Fresh crabmeat should be dated, or you should ask the fishmonger how long it will last. If buying canned products, make sure that the can isn't rusty or dented.

Sometimes, certain fish may not be available, but that doesn't mean you can't make a recipe. Ask the fishmonger to recommend a good substitute.

Preparing Fish and Shellfish

This section tells you how to prepare various types of fish and shellfish for soup.

Frozen fish

If you don't live near a large body of water, you're probably not going to work with fresh fish as much as you would like, but don't despair. Quality frozen fish will taste just as good in soup.

You should thaw frozen fish at room temperature for about half an hour, then cook it immediately. The partially frozen fish will remain more moist and tender in your recipe than if you let it thaw completely. Because the fish will be partially frozen, you'll need to increase the cooking time by one third to one half. For example, if fresh or fully thawed fish takes 10 minutes to cook, you need to cook semi-thawed fish for 12 to 15 minutes.

Fresh clams

Cook live shellfish with tightly closed shells, and discard any that doesn't open when cooked (see Figure 12-1). For the soup recipes in this book, use hard shell clams or quahogs. Scrub clams well with a wire brush. Let the clams sit in a sink or basin filled with cold water for 20 to 30 minutes so that they spit out any sand or grit. Don't let them stand longer or they'll die, which will make them inedible.

Figure 12-1:
Closed and
open clams.

To cook fresh clams, bring 1½ cups water to a boil in a large Dutch oven or pot. Add the clams and reduce the heat to medium-low. Cover and simmer until the clam shells open, about 5 minutes. Remove the clams with a slotted spoon and discard any that did not open. Strain the cooking liquid and reserve to use as broth. For the chowder recipes in this book, remove the clams from their shells and set aside.

Fresh mussels

Scrub mussels well with a wire brush. Fill a basin or sink with cold water and add a couple of generous pinches of flour or cornmeal. Let the mussels soak in this water for 30 to 60 minutes, but no longer or they'll die. (Then you'd have to discard them.) Rinse well. Pull or cut off the beard (the tough threads that the mussel uses to attach itself to rocks) as shown in Figure 12-2.

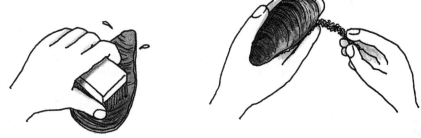

Figure 12-2:
Cleaning a
mussel.

To cook fresh mussels, bring 1½ cups water or ¾ cup water and ¾ cup white wine to a boil in a large pot. Add the mussels and reduce the heat to medium-low. Cover and simmer until the mussel shells open, about 5 minutes. Remove the mussels with a slotted spoon and discard any that did not open. Strain the cooking liquid and reserve to use as part of the broth. For soup recipes, remove the mussels from their shells and set aside, but keep a few in the shell to use as a garnish.

Fresh shrimp

Shrimp needs to be deveined before using. To devein shrimp, first peel them. With a sharp paring knife, make a shallow slit along the back of the shrimp. With the tip of the knife, loosen, remove, and discard the dark vein, as shown in Figure 12-3.

Wash any utensils that you've used in preparing raw seafood, such as cutting boards and knives, with hot, soapy water.

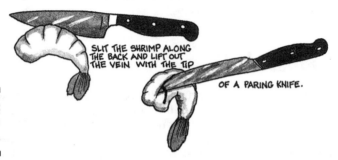

Figure 12-3:
Deveining a shrimp.

Creating Seafood Chowders and Bisques

Bisques are rich creamy soups most often made with pureed or finely chopped seafood, although sometimes vegetables such as tomatoes are used to make a bisque. Chowders are all-American soups that are rich, thick, and chunky. You'll find other, more ethnic fish and shellfish soups, in Chapter 14.

Chowders are best when freshly made, but bisques can be frozen and reheated.

The quality of a fish soup depends on the quality of fish broth used. Try to make your own — you can do it in about 30 minutes. See the recipe for Fish Broths and Shrimp Broth in Chapter 5. Good chicken broth or vegetable broth is preferable to a poor fish broth.

Chowders: An American favorite

Chowder's roots lie in colonial New England's seafaring towns where it's still standard fare at dockside and city restaurants. The name, however, is a French import — *chowder* is a derivative of the words *chaudière,* meaning "steaming boiler," or *chaudron,* meaning "cauldron." Both evoke the image of a piping hot pot of soup. Chowders were originally made of staples — onions, salt pork, milk or cream, and fish or clams, and thickened with cracker-type sea biscuits or bread. Eventually, the potato replaced biscuits as the thickener. Now, we serve crackers on the side. Tomatoes crept in, creating Manhattan-style versions, much to the dismay of chowder purists. Today, the chowder category also includes hearty corn soups.

Fresh Salmon Chowder

This luxurious soup has become a standard in the Pacific Northwest, where fresh salmon is abundant.

Yield: *4 to 6 servings*

Level: *Easy*

Preparation time: *10 to 15 minutes*

Cooking time: *50 to 60 minutes*

Do not freeze

2 tablespoons butter or margarine

3 medium leeks, white part only, sliced

1 medium onion, chopped

1 tablespoon tomato paste

½ cup dry white wine or vermouth

2½ cups homemade fish, vegetable, or chicken broth

2 cups half-and-half or light cream

1 large potato, about 6 to 8 ounces, peeled and diced

1 bay leaf

1 teaspoon paprika

12 to 14 ounce fresh, boneless, skinless salmon filet, cut into 1-inch chunks

Salt to taste, about ½ teaspoon

½ teaspoon freshly ground black pepper

1 tablespoon chopped fresh parsley, chives, or dill

1 In a large pot over medium heat, melt the butter. Add the leeks and onion and sauté until very tender, about 10 minutes.

2 Add the tomato paste and cook, stirring for 1 minute. Add the wine and cook, stirring for 2 minutes. Add the broth, half-and-half, potato, bay leaf, and paprika. Simmer, partially covered, until the potatoes are tender, about 25 to 30 minutes.

3 Reduce the heat to medium-low. Add the salmon and simmer until it is cooked through, about 5 to 7 minutes.

4 Remove the bay leaf. Season with salt, pepper, and herbs. Serve immediately, garnished with additional parsley, chives, or dill.

Per Serving: *Calories 263.9; Protein 15.7g; Carbohydrates 15.7g; Dietary fiber 1.6g; Total fat 15.8g; Saturated fat 8.8g; Cholesterol 69.5mg; Sodium 320.0mg.*

Fisherman's Chowder

Use whatever firm fish is freshly available in your market. Serve with plenty of crackers or perhaps the traditional oyster cracker on the side.

Do not use soft-textured fish, such as flounder, sole, sea bass, redfish, or trout because they tend to fall apart. Any firmer-textured fish will work well.

Yield: *6 servings*

Level: *Easy*

Preparation time: *10 to 15 minutes*

Cooking time: *45 to 55 minutes*

Do not freeze

3 tablespoons butter or margarine

1 medium onion, chopped

1 celery stalk, chopped

1 medium carrot, finely diced

2 plump cloves garlic, minced

3 cups homemade fish or chicken broth

2 medium potatoes, about 12 ounces, peeled and diced

1 bay leaf

1½ teaspoons minced fresh thyme, or ¾ teaspoon dried thyme

1½ to 1¾ cups half-and-half, cream, or milk

1¼ pounds firm, boneless, skinless white fish filets, such as monkfish, cod, haddock, or catfish, cut in 1½-inch cubes

Salt to taste, about ½ teaspoon

¼ teaspoon freshly ground black pepper

2 tablespoons chopped fresh parsley

1 In a large pot over medium heat, melt the butter. Add the onion, celery, and carrot and sauté, stirring occasionally, until the vegetables are nearly tender, about 10 minutes. Add the garlic and cook, stirring often, for about 2 minutes.

2 Add the broth, potatoes, bay leaf, and thyme. Cover and simmer until the potatoes are tender, about 20 to 25 minutes.

3 Add the half-and-half and fish. Simmer, uncovered, until the fish is cooked through, about 5 to 7 minutes.

4 Season with salt and pepper. Stir in the parsley.

Per Serving: *Calories 291.7; Protein 23.5g; Carbohydrates 17.5g; Dietary fiber 1.9g; Total fat 14.2g; Saturated fat 8.4g; Cholesterol 78.2mg; Sodium 362.2mg.*

Manhattan Clam Chowder

More than just an island in the Hudson, Manhattan is also the tomato-based chowder that sparks a heated debate between its devotees and New England Chowder lovers. The verdict is in: It's a darn good soup.

Yield: *6 to 8 servings*

Level: *Easy to intermediate (depending on whether you're using fresh clams)*

Preparation time: *15 minutes (or 25 minutes if using fresh clams)*

Cooking time: *40 minutes*

Do not freeze

2 tablespoons olive oil

1 medium onion, chopped

1 celery stalk, diced

½ medium green bell pepper, diced

One 28-ounce can plum tomatoes with juice, broken with the back of a wooden spoon

3½ cups clam or fish broth, or 1½ cups clam juice and 2 cups water

2 medium potatoes, peeled and diced

1 teaspoon minced fresh thyme, or ½ teaspoon dried thyme

1 teaspoon minced fresh basil, or ½ teaspoon dried basil

¼ teaspoon minced fresh oregano, or ⅛ teaspoon dried oregano

1 bay leaf

Two 6½-ounce cans clams with juice reserved for broth, or 1 to 1½ cups fresh cooked clams, removed from their shells, about 3 to 4 dozen clams

Salt to taste, about ½ to ¾ teaspoon

½ teaspoon freshly ground black pepper

2 tablespoons minced fresh parsley

1 In a large pot over medium heat, heat the olive oil. Add the onion, celery, and bell pepper and sauté, stirring occasionally, until the vegetables are tender, about 10 minutes.

2 Add the tomatoes, broth, potatoes, thyme, basil, oregano, and bay leaf. Cover partially and simmer until the potatoes are tender, about 20 to 25 minutes.

3 Add the clams and cook until the clams are heated through, about 5 minutes. Remove the bay leaf. Season with salt and pepper and stir in the parsley.

Per Serving: Calories 139.0; Protein 8.5g; Carbohydrates 17.0g; Dietary fiber 2.4g; Total fat 4.7g; Saturated fat 0.9g; Cholesterol 15.1mg; Sodium 374.5mg.

New England Clam Chowder

This, the most famous of all chowders, originally comes from the Massachusetts coast. I've given instructions for both fresh and canned clams because folks who live inland don't always have access to fresh. Serve with crackers or oyster crackers.

Yield: *8 servings*

Level: *Easy to intermediate (depending on whether you're using fresh clams)*

Preparation time: *15 minutes (or 25 if using fresh clams)*

Cooking time: *45 to 55 minutes*

Do not freeze

2 to 3 strips bacon, diced

1 medium onion, chopped

2 cups milk

1 cup clam or fish broth, or $\frac{1}{2}$ cup clam juice and $\frac{1}{2}$ cup water, or reserved canned clam liquid, thinned with water to make 1 cup

2 medium potatoes, about 12 ounces, peeled and diced

1 bay leaf

$\frac{1}{2}$ teaspoon minced fresh thyme leaves, or $\frac{1}{4}$ teaspoon dried thyme

$\frac{1}{2}$ to 1 cup cream

Two 6$\frac{1}{2}$-ounce cans clams with juice reserved for broth, or 1 to 1$\frac{1}{2}$ cups fresh cooked clams removed from their shells, about 3 to 4 dozen

Salt to taste, about $\frac{1}{2}$ teaspoon

$\frac{1}{2}$ teaspoon freshly ground black pepper

2 tablespoons chopped fresh parsley

1 In a large pot over medium-low heat, cook the bacon, stirring occasionally, until the fat is rendered and the bacon is nearly cooked through. Add the onion and sauté, stirring occasionally, until translucent, about 5 to 7 minutes.

2 Add the milk, clam broth, potatoes, bay leaf, and thyme. Cover partially and simmer until the potatoes are tender, about 20 to 25 minutes. Do not allow the liquid to boil.

3 Add the cream and clams and cook, uncovered, until the clams are heated through, about 5 minutes.

4 Remove the bay leaf. Season with salt and pepper. Stir in the parsley.

Variation: *Reduced-fat New England Clam Chowder: Replace the bacon with 1$\frac{1}{2}$ tablespoons vegetable oil and $\frac{1}{4}$ to $\frac{1}{3}$ cup chopped ham or Canadian bacon. To start the soup, heat the vegetable oil, and then add the ham or Canadian bacon and onion. Sauté until the onion is translucent, about 5 minutes. Continue with the recipe, but substitute milk for the cream.*

Tip: *Use hard shell clams or quahogs for the clam chowder recipes in this book. Try to buy littleneck clams, which are small. If the clams are large, such as cherrystone, chop them coarsely after they're cooked.*

Per Serving: Calories 187.4; Protein 10.1g; Carbohydrates 13.2g; Dietary fiber 1.0g; Total fat 10.5g; Saturated fat 5.7g; Cholesterol 46.6mg; Sodium 296.8mg.

Easy Lobster Bisque

This extravagant soup featuring lobster and cream is decadently rich and absolutely delicious. Fresh, cooked lobster meat is available in many seafood departments of supermarkets and fish shops.

Yield: *4 to 6 servings*

Level: *Easy*

Preparation time: *10 to 15 minutes*

Cooking time: *30 minutes*

Freezes well

3 tablespoons butter or margarine

4 scallions, white part only, chopped

¾ teaspoon paprika

3 tablespoons all-purpose flour

2⅓ cups milk, heated

2 tablespoons dry white vermouth, or 1 tablespoon bourbon

½ teaspoon Worcestershire sauce

12 ounces cooked lobster meat, chopped or shredded

⅔ to 1 cup cream or half-and-half

Salt to taste, about ½ teaspoon

⅛ teaspoon white pepper

1 In a large pot over medium heat, melt the butter. Add the scallions and sauté, stirring occasionally, until tender, about 5 minutes. Stir in the paprika.

2 Add the flour and cook, stirring constantly, for 2 to 3 minutes.

3 Gradually add the milk, stirring or whisking often until smooth. Add the vermouth and Worcestershire sauce and stir to blend. Simmer, uncovered, for 10 minutes.

4 Add the lobster and simmer, uncovered, for 5 minutes.

5 Add the cream and simmer until heated through, about 5 minutes. Do not allow the soup to boil. Season with salt and white pepper.

Per Serving: Calories 271.6; Protein 15.7g; Carbohydrates 9.4g; Dietary fiber 0.3g; Total fat 19.2g; Saturated fat 11.7g; Cholesterol 105.4mg; Sodium 472.5mg.

Easy Crab Bisque

A famous South Carolina soup, She-Crab Soup, uses both the crabmeat and its roe. Traditionally, the roe gives the soup its characteristic pale pink color, but it is not always available. In this recipe, a little paprika does the trick.

Yield: *6 servings*

Level: *Easy*

Preparation time: *10 to 15 minutes*

Cooking time: *30 minutes*

Freezes well

3 tablespoons butter or margarine

4 scallions, white part only, chopped

½ teaspoon paprika

3 tablespoons all-purpose flour

2⅓ cups milk, heated

2 tablespoons dry sherry

½ teaspoon Worcestershire sauce

12 ounces fresh lump crabmeat, picked over, or two 6-ounce cans, drained

⅔ to 1 cup cream or half-and-half

Salt to taste, about ½ teaspoon

⅛ teaspoon white pepper

⅛ to ¼ teaspoon cayenne

1 In a large pot over medium heat, melt the butter. Add the scallions and sauté, stirring occasionally, until tender, about 5 minutes. Stir in the paprika.

2 Add the flour and cook, stirring constantly, for 2 to 3 minutes.

3 Gradually add the milk, stirring or whisking often until smooth. Add the sherry and Worcestershire sauce and stir to blend. Simmer, uncovered, for 10 minutes.

4 Add the crabmeat and simmer, uncovered, for 5 minutes.

5 Add the cream and heat for 5 minutes. Do not allow the soup to boil. Season with salt, white pepper, and cayenne.

Caution: *Although it's been cleaned and picked by packers, you should pick over fresh lump crabmeat to remove any extraneous bits of shell that would spoil the soup.*

Cook's Fact: *Manufacturers say that surimi, a processed form of white fish (generally pollack), is a replacement for crab. However, it is not suitable for this soup.*

Per Serving: *Calories 228.5; Protein 18.0g; Carbohydrates 9.1g; Dietary fiber 0.3g; Total fat 12.8g; Saturated fat 7.5g; Cholesterol 99.1mg; Sodium 473.5mg.*

Barbara's Canned Salmon Bisque

Easy to prepare, this creamy soup utilizes staple ingredients.

Yield: 4 to 6 servings

Tools: Food processor, blender, or hand blender

Preparation time: 10 minutes

Cooking time: 40 to 50 minutes

Freezes well

2 tablespoons butter or margarine

3 medium leeks, white part only, sliced

1 medium onion, chopped

1 tablespoon tomato paste

½ cup dry white wine or vermouth

2½ cups homemade fish, vegetable, or chicken broth

2 cups half-and-half or milk

1 large potato, about 6 to 8 ounces, peeled and diced

1 bay leaf

1 teaspoon paprika

12 to 14 ounces canned salmon, drained

Salt to taste, about ½ teaspoon

½ teaspoon freshly ground black pepper

1 tablespoon chopped fresh parsley, chives, or dill

1 In a large pot over medium heat, melt the butter. Add the leeks and onion, and sauté until very tender, about 10 minutes.

2 Add the tomato paste and cook, stirring constantly for 1 minute. Add the wine and cook, stirring, for 2 minutes.

3 Add the broth, half-and-half, potato, bay leaf, and paprika. Simmer, partially covered, until the potatoes are tender, about 25 to 30 minutes.

4 Reduce the heat to medium-low. Add the salmon and heat through, about 5 to 7 minutes.

5 Remove the bay leaf. Puree in batches in a blender or food processor until a chunky puree forms. Alternatively, if you have a hand blender, leave the soup in the pot and blend to a chunky consistency.

6 Return the soup to the pot and reheat over medium heat. Season with salt and pepper. Serve garnished with parsley, chives, or dill.

Cook'sFact: High in protein, salmon is a good source of vitamins A and B, as well as omega 3 fatty acids.

Per Serving: Calories 232.8; Protein 14.7g; Carbohydrates 20.0g; Dietary fiber 2.0g; Total fat 11.2g; Saturated fat 5.4g; Cholesterol 52.8mg; Sodium 498.2mg.

Part IV
Souping Up

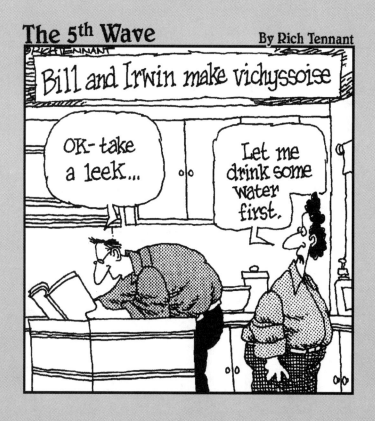

In this part . . .

The chapters in this section give you all the information you need to go global and experience a wide range of international tastes. You'll find out how to enhance flavor with both herbs and spices as well as discover the ingredients and seasonings used in a variety of ethnic cooking styles. Recipes include classic regional soups and several popular and refreshing cold soups.

Chapter 13

Season It!

*W*e have widened our culinary horizons to take advantage of tastes from around the world, and today's food is bursting with flavor. Present-day cooks have a broader culinary repertoire, encompassing family favorites as well as regional specialties. The popularity of a wide range of ethnic dishes has transformed formerly exotic seasonings, such as allspice, cumin, fresh basil, fresh cilantro, and sesame oil, into everyday items that are available in most supermarkets.

Learning how to season correctly is an art that requires knowledge, patience, and the courage to indulge in a bit of experimentation. Follow these helpful hints to begin your quest:

- When using a new herb or spice, become familiar with it — smell it and taste it on the tip of your tongue.

- Start with the amount a recipe calls for — flavors can concentrate during the cooking process and too much can easily overpower a dish. If you want to add more next time, make any increases in small increments.

- Always salt soup or broth near or at the end of the cooking time.

- Spices should be added toward the beginning of the cooking process.

- Herbs can be added in the beginning and during the cooking time. Some herbs are stirred in right before serving.

- When garnishing with herbs, always use fresh.

Spicy places

Although most spices originally hail from Asia and the Indonesian Spice Islands, the Far East doesn't have a monopoly. Some spices have traveled and are now grown elsewhere — ginger in Jamaica and Nigeria, cloves in Zanzibar and Madagascar, and nutmeg in Grenada. Hot chilies, a popular seasoning native to the Americas, made their way around the globe and are used from Mexico to Asia, either fresh, dried, or ground.

Spices

Highly valued throughout the ages for their culinary and medicinal properties, spices are aromatic seasonings — the seeds, roots, fruits, flowers, or bark of a variety of tropical trees and plants. This prized commodity used in food, perfume, medicine, ceremonies, and religious rites could buy freedom for a medieval serf. Spices sparked Columbus' search for an alternate route to the East Indies and his subsequent westward voyage to America. Except for fresh garlic, ginger, chilies, lemon grass, and lime leaves, spices are always used dried. Spices can be found in markets either whole or ground.

Buying spices

Ground spices have a six month shelf life after they're opened before their potency diminishes dramatically. It's best to buy them as you need them and in small quantities. If you use a particular spice often, then by all means buy a larger amount; otherwise, buy small amounts and replenish periodically. Whole spices will last longer, up to a year or more, and you can grind them yourself. Figure 13-1 shows a variety of spices.

Figure 13-1: Spices galore.

CUMIN SEEDS

CINNAMON STICK

CORIANDER SEEDS

FENNEL SEEDS

CARDAMOM SEEDS

BLACK PEPPERCORNS

Toasting and grinding spices

Some whole spices such as cumin, coriander, and fennel seeds benefit from light toasting before grinding. This process releases more of the natural aroma, oils, and flavor. Grind whole spices, with or without toasting first, in a mini food processor or small spice or coffee mill that you use for that purpose (see Figure 13-2). Try to grind them as you need them, but you can store home-ground spices in a tightly sealed jar. Unless you're very experienced and can tell them apart by color and smell, make sure that you label the container.

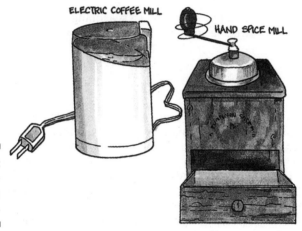

ELECTRIC COFFEE MILL

HAND SPICE MILL

Figure 13-2:
Spice-
grinding
implements.

 To bring out the flavor of spices, toast them briefly before using. To toast spices, heat them in a heated, dry skillet over medium heat until slightly browned and fragrant, just a few moments. Toss them or stir them occasionally while they're in the pan so they don't burn and remove them from the hot pan as soon as they're toasted. Burned spices have an unpleasant taste and must be thrown out.

 Buy herbs and spices as you need them, in amounts that you can use in about six months.

 If you buy whole nutmeg, don't try to grind it. Use a nutmeg grater or the finest side of a four-sided grater.

Storing spices

Keep spices in a sealed glass or plastic container in a cool, dark place, away from heat, preferably not above the stove or the oven. Make sure you store them on their own or with canned goods. Some foods, such as chocolate and rice, absorb the flavor of the spices. Who wants to munch on curried chocolate?

Superstar Seasonings

You'll want to make sure that you have these seasonings on hand. They'll mean the difference between a so-so soup and a *souper* soup!

Salt

Salt is used more often and in more foods than any other ingredient, and it doubles as both a flavoring agent and a preservative. Treasured throughout history for its amazing properties, salt marries the individual elements in a dish. Food without salt often seems to be lacking the proverbial "something." Even a small amount blends and unifies tastes in a dish that otherwise seems unfinished. The only trick is to use it sparingly. Start by adding a small amount, stir well, then taste, and carefully add more if you want. In the soup recipes in this book, begin with ½ teaspoon. If you want to be more cautious or have used a salty commercial broth, taste first, and if you need to season, start with ¼ teaspoon.

Kosher salt has a medium grain and is the top choice of many chefs for cooking. Sea salt comes in medium and fine grain, and can be used like common table salt. Either is excellent for general cooking. When baking, always use common table salt because it's finely ground.

Pepper

Pepper is one of world's most popular seasoning, adding an aromatic sharpness to food. Black pepper is the most common, and several varieties are available: bold flavored tellichery, pungent and hot Brazilian, and smooth and balanced Malabar. When you buy whole peppercorns, the type is often listed on the label. Other kinds of pepper used in cooking include the milder white pepper and mixed peppercorn blends of white, black, pink, and green.

Ground pepper loses its character within a couple of months, so it's wise to buy it whole. Make sure that you also buy a peppermill for black peppercorns so you can grind it fresh. If you want to grind different varieties regularly, it's more convenient to have a separate mill for each kind than to empty a mill and get rid of the pepper residue each time you want to change the kind or color of peppercorns. Sometimes, one type of pepper isn't completely out of the mechanism when you grind another kind.

Cameo Roles

They're small, but they're vital. Garlic, ginger, chilies, and lemon grass are sold fresh in the produce section of your market. They are the primary flavor underpinning many cuisines and are used extensively in soups.

Garlic

Garlic, a cousin of onions and leeks, is sold in whole heads comprised of separate cloves. Store it in a cool, dark, and dry place, away from other food. I generally keep mine with onions.

Heads should keep for a month or two, whereas individual cloves will stay fresh for about two weeks. Discard any shriveled, discolored, or sprouting cloves.

Cloves can be of varying sizes from plump to small, depending on whether they're from the exterior or inner core. When a recipe calls for a clove of garlic, it refers to a plump one. You may need to use two to three of the small ones to get the equivalent amount. Bottled, chopped garlic and peeled whole cloves are available in many refrigerator cases in markets and should be stored in the fridge at home. Always use fresh because the dried is a poor alternative, lacking its pungent character.

Most often, garlic is added to onions or other aromatic vegetables that have already been softened. When cooking garlic, make sure that you have enough oil, cook over medium-low to medium heat, and stir frequently. You must take care that the garlic doesn't burn because it will acquire an unpleasantly acrid taste that can ruin an entire dish. If it burns, you'll have to discard the lot, not only the garlic but also the veggies cooked with it, and start afresh.

To peel cloves easily, put the flat side of a kitchen knife on the clove and tap the knife gently, but firmly. The skin should break and peel easily. Be careful not to smash the garlic, which makes it more prone to burning.

These measurement equivalents may come in handy:

- 1 plump clove garlic = ½ teaspoon minced, fresh garlic
- 1 inch piece ginger = 1 tablespoon minced, fresh ginger

Ginger

Always use fresh ginger in soups. Dried ginger has a different taste and is not a substitute in cooking, although it is wonderful for many baked goods. Buy ginger that has a strong fragrance and is firm, with smooth, unwrinkled skin. Unpeeled, it should last for 2 to 3 weeks in the refrigerator. Remember to peel the ginger before grating or mincing.

Fresh chilies

Numerous types of fresh chilies can be found in most produce sections (see Figure 13-3). Although, I frequently use jalapeños, cayenne, and serranos, use one that you prefer. Whether fresh or dried, chilies need to be handled carefully because they can burn your skin, eyes, and mouth.

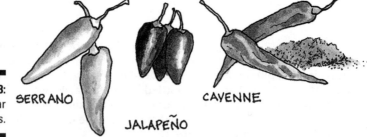

Figure 13-3:
Popular chilies.

SERRANO

JALAPEÑO

CAYENNE

Always wash your hands well after touching chilies or chili seeds. Keep your fingers away from your face and eyes. For extra protection, wear thin rubber or latex gloves to prevent skin irritation when handling chilies.

The heat of a chili can and does vary, even within a particular variety. Some jalapeños are very hot and others are relatively mild. You might want to taste a tiny sliver to decide how much you want to use before you add it to a dish. To reduce the heat a bit, remove the ribs, as well as the seeds, from the chili. In many recipes, a quantity range is given such as 1 to 2 jalapeños, taking into account their fluctuating "heat" factor. If you prefer a hint of chili, use less than the recipes call for. You know what to do if you want it hotter.

Lemon grass and lime leaves

Native to Southeast Asia and a central ingredient in Thai and Vietnamese cuisine, lemon grass and lime leaves can be purchased in Asian groceries and in the ethnic sections of supermarkets and specialty stores.

Lemon grass stalks are available fresh or dried. Fresh (shown in Figure 13-4) is preferable, but 1 stalk is roughly equivalent to 1½ to 2 tablespoons dried and chopped. Because the dried is less potent, the exchange ratio is not equal.

Figure 13-4:
Fresh lemon
grass.

Thai lime leaves, also called kaffir lime leaves, are from the makrud tree. They are available either fresh or dried. If you use dried, their flavor is less intense, and you might want to use an extra leaf or two.

Herbs

Herbs bring another dimension to food, subtly enhancing its flavor and or graciously garnishing its appearance. Like spices, herbs have historically been used in cooking, medicines, and rituals. Herbs, the leafy part of plants and trees, though widely marketed in dried form, are increasingly available fresh in produce aisles. I show a bunch of them in Figure 13-5. Many people use dried as a matter of convenience, but some herbs should always be used fresh because their distinctive aroma and taste are completely lost when dried. These include the everyday favorites of parsley, cilantro, dill, and mint, as well as less commonplace chervil and sage. Basil, in particular, should be used fresh, because dried basil barely even resembles the fresh in flavor. Dried herbs have a longer shelf life than fresh, about 6 to 8 months for commercially dried and up to a year for home-dried.

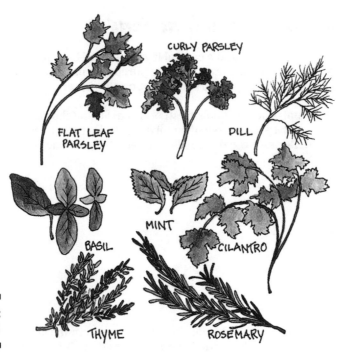

Figure 13-5:
Herbs!

If you have a green thumb, grow your own herbs in a small garden, in pots on the stoop or patio, or in window boxes. After you've used fresh ones, you'll notice the difference and want to use them whenever possible. This is especially true with parsley, basil, cilantro, dill, and mint.

Storing fresh herbs

Keep fresh herbs in the refrigerator because they are highly perishable, but remove any decaying leaves before storing. Wrap them gently in a lightly dampened, but not wet, paper towel. If the leaves are too wet, they will spoil quickly. Put the bundle in a plastic bag, wrap it loosely in plastic wrap, or put it in a sealable plastic container. Parsley, cilantro, and mint can also be stored in the refrigerator with stems down in a small cup of water. You can cover the leafy top loosely with a plastic bag.

Washing and chopping fresh herbs

Before using herbs, look and taste to see if they are dirty. Sometimes, they are well washed before you buy them and are sold in sealed plastic containers. Rinse them under cold running water, shake them gently over the sink to get rid of excess water, and pat them dry with a paper towel.

Use only leaves that look fresh. Discard any yellowed, slimy, or blemished leaves from herbs as parsley, basil, mint, and cilantro. Don't use the stems of herbs (including parsley). Gently separate leaves from stems so they don't become bruised. The exception is cilantro; its thin stems (and occasionally even the roots) are chopped in Thai cuisine. Dill should not be chopped. With a pair of scissors, snip its feathery fronds from the stem into small pieces.

When herbs are to be chopped for cooking, they should be minced or chopped finely. The only exception is when whole herbs are specifically called for, such as in a bouquet garni and for garnishes, where small sprigs or whole leaves are more visually appealing accents.

Making a bouquet garni

Traditionally, a bouquet garni is a small bunch of herbs — parsley, thyme, and bay leaf — tied together, wrapped in a piece of cheesecloth, or in the outer layer of a leek. It's added to a dish to augment its flavor. Tying the herbs together makes it easier to remove from a finished dish. Now bouquets garnis often include other herb and spice combinations.

BOUQUET GARNI

Figure 13-6:
Making a
bouquet
garni.

Drying fresh herbs

If you have too much of a fresh herb, whether from your garden or left over from a market purchase, you can dry it so it doesn't go to waste. Home-dried herbs are still "fresher," and thus tastier, than commercially dried. Rinse the herbs and pat dry. Leave cleaned herbs out to air dry, preferably tied together in bunches and hanging upside down. They should be dry within a few days. When you're certain that they are completely dry, remove the leaves from the stalks and crush. Store home-dried herbs in a covered container for up to a year.

Chapter 14

The Melting Pot

*N*ations become known for their delicious ethnic specialties, and this includes soup. Some are filling enough to be a main dish, while others are light enough to be served as starters. Many of the best soups on America's tables are popular classics of other countries. Get out your soup pot and embark a culinary tour.

When you're designing the entire menu under one ethnic theme or featuring one ethnic dish, keep the rest of the menu simple.

Global Village Mix 'n' Match: Using Regional Ingredients and Flavors

Many ingredients — such as meat, poultry, fish, onions, carrots, and celery — are universal, and others are specific to certain countries or regions. Most cuisines combine certain items regularly, and drawing on flavorings from specific places can help bring the whole world to your table.

This useful guide offers suggestions for mixing foods and seasonings according to their ethnic heritage, whether you're being creative with just one recipe or planning an entire menu.

Northern Europe

This list will help you discover and use the favorite flavors and ingredients of northern European countries:

- **Scandinavia:** sour cream, cream, butter, dill, nutmeg, cardamom, ginger, cheeses, anchovies, pickled foods, and beets

- **Russia, Poland, and Ukraine:** sour cream, beets, cabbage, potatoes, caraway, vinegar, mustard, and kielbasa or sausage

- **Hungary:** sour cream, butter, paprika, marjoram, and vinegar

- **Germany:** butter, potatoes, cabbage, cheeses, beer, caraway, nutmeg, beets, and vinegar

- **Holland and Belgium:** butter, cream, Gouda and Edam cheeses, chervil, parsley, and beer

- **United Kingdom:** butter, cream, Stilton blue and Cheddar cheeses, dried fish, and potatoes

- **Northern France:** butter, cream, cheeses, flat-leaf parsley, wine, and beer

The Mediterranean

This list will help you discover and use the favorite flavors and ingredients of Mediterranean countries:

- **Provence (southern France):** wine, olive oil, garlic, thyme, tarragon, flat-leaf parsley, rosemary, basil, almonds, Parmesan cheese, pasta, black olives, roasted red peppers, tomatoes, oranges, lemons, and white beans

- **Greece:** olive oil, garlic, oregano, lemons, black olives, and tomatoes

- **Italy:** wine, olive oil, garlic, flat-leaf parsley, basil, rosemary, pasta, polenta, hazelnuts, Parmesan and Romano cheeses, balsamic vinegar, anchovies, black olives, roasted red peppers, tomatoes, almonds, oranges, lemons, and white beans

- **Spain:** sherry, olive oil, green and black olives, garlic, bell peppers, tomatoes, chili peppers, and paprika

- **Portugal:** port wine, chorizo, olive oil, chili peppers, and paprika

- **Morocco:** cinnamon, cumin, honey, lemons, oranges, chickpeas, tomatoes, saffron, and cloves

The Americas

This list will help you discover and use the favorite flavors and ingredients of countries of the Americas:

- **United States and Canada:** cranberries, wild rice, corn, maple syrup, turkey, clams, lobster, salmon, butternut squash, and pumpkins

- **Southern United States:** collard greens, sweet potatoes, peanuts, pecans, lima beans, corn, vinegar, whiskey, hominy, and cornmeal

- **Cajun and Creole:** scallions, onions, bell peppers, celery, tomatoes, andouille sausage, Tabasco sauce, white pepper, cayenne, thyme, bay leaf, red beans, parsley, and shrimp

- **Southwestern United States:** chili powder, chili peppers, tomatoes, corn, cornmeal, beans, cilantro, oregano, garlic, and cumin

- **Mexico:** chili peppers, almonds, chocolate, tomatoes, vanilla, sesame seeds, corn, cornmeal, beans, limes, avocados, butternut squash, cilantro, garlic, chorizo, oregano, cumin, and turkey

- **Caribbean:** Scotch Bonnet peppers, coconuts, mangos, papayas, rum, allspice, clove, cinnamon, thyme, ginger, garlic, sweet potatoes, pumpkins, and rice

- **South America:** chili peppers, yams, peanuts, cumin, paprika, bell peppers, corn, potatoes, and black beans

Africa

This list will help you discover and use the favorite flavors and ingredients of African regions:

- **West Africa:** pumpkins, sweet potatoes, peanuts, chili peppers, collards, garlic, and beans

- **South Africa:** wine, chili peppers, vinegar, cinnamon, allspice, clove, coriander, curry powder, cumin, bay leaf, ginger, garlic, coconut milk, mint, cilantro, butternut squash, tomatoes, corn, hominy, rice, oranges, tangerines

Asia

This list will help you discover and use the favorite flavors and ingredients of Asian countries:

- ✔ **India:** chili peppers, ginger, garlic, cinnamon, clove, turmeric, coriander, curry powder, garam masala, cumin, bay leaf, tomatoes, coconuts, mint, cilantro, and rice

- ✔ **Thailand:** lemon grass, garlic, ginger, chili peppers, fish sauce, holy basil, mint, cilantro, rice, and scallions

- ✔ **Malaysia and Indonesia:** chili peppers, coconuts, mangos, papayas, brown sugar, vinegar, cilantro, soy sauce, cinnamon, cardamom, clove, coriander, bay leaf, ginger, garlic, mint, cilantro, and rice

- ✔ **China:** soy sauce, ginger, garlic, scallions, rice, egg and rice noodles, wood or cloud ear mushrooms, hoisin sauce, oyster sauce, sesame oil, and chili oil

- ✔ **Japan:** soy sauce, daikon, miso, rice wine, rice wine vinegar, rice, rice noodles, udon noodles, mung bean noodles, ginger, garlic, and scallions

When improvising, keep your dish or menu uncomplicated and simple. Combine flavors from the same ethnic background.

Soups from the Melting Pot

Reflecting America's diverse ethnicity and culinary tastes, this varied collection presents treasured recipes from around the world. Ladle up a classic from France, Italy, Russia, Japan, China, Indonesia, India, or Africa.

Spanish Garlic Soup with Cheese Dumplings

Garlic soup hails from Spain. Many versions are topped with eggs that are poached in the soup. Although not traditional, I add flavorful Parmesan and cornmeal dumplings that are simmered briefly in the soup.

When measuring the cornmeal, stir it first, then spoon it into a measuring cup and level off.

Yield: *6 servings*

Level: *Intermediate*

Preparation time: *20 to 25 minutes*

Standing time: *25 to 30 minutes*

Cooking time: *40 to 50 minutes*

Freezes well

For the dumplings

½ cup fine white or yellow cornmeal

½ cup freshly grated Parmesan or Romano cheese

¼ teaspoon salt

⅛ to ¼ teaspoon cayenne pepper

⅛ teaspoon white pepper

2 teaspoons finely grated onion

1 tablespoon finely minced parsley

2 ½ tablespoons butter, melted

1 large egg plus 1 egg white, lightly beaten

For the garlic soup:

2 tablespoons olive oil

14 to 18 plump cloves garlic, peeled

6 cups chicken broth

Salt to taste, about ½ teaspoon

¼ teaspoon freshly ground white or black pepper, or to taste

1 **To prepare the dumplings:** In a small bowl, combine the cornmeal, cheese, salt, cayenne, and pepper. Add the onion and parsley and stir to mix. With a fork, blend in the butter. Make a well in the center of the dry ingredients. Add the egg and stir with a fork. Knead the dough briefly in the bowl until a smooth dough forms, about 1 to 2 minutes.

2 Let the dough rest for 25 to 30 minutes. Form the dough into a rectangle and score evenly with a knife into 18 pieces. Form the pieces into small balls by rolling them gently in the palm of your hand. Cover loosely with a clean kitchen towel or plastic wrap to prevent them from drying out. Set aside at room temperature.

3 **To prepare the soup:** In a medium pot over medium-low heat, heat the olive oil. Add the garlic and cook, turning the cloves once or twice, until they just begin to turn lightly golden, about 5 to 7 minutes. Add the chicken broth, cover, and simmer for 20 to 25 minutes.

4 Remove the garlic cloves with a skimmer or slotted spoon. Puree the garlic with 2 to 3 tablespoons of the hot broth in a food processor or blender, or mash well with a fork. Return the garlic puree to the broth. Season with salt and pepper.

5 **To cook the dumplings:** Bring the broth to a gentle simmer over medium-low to medium heat. Add the dumplings to the broth. Simmer, uncovered, until they are cooked, about 10 minutes. Do not allow the broth to boil vigorously or the dumplings may fall apart.

Tip: *To remove all the garlic puree from the food processor or blender, ladle a small amount of broth into the container. With a small spoon, scrape any remaining garlic into the broth, and then return the broth to the pot.*

Per Serving: *Calories 217.6; Protein 7.0g; Carbohydrates 11.9g; Dietary fiber 1.1g; Total fat 15.9g; Saturated fat 5.9g; Cholesterol 57.3mg; Sodium 1457.7mg.*

French Onion Soup

This soup, topped with toasted bread and cheese, is a superb winter entree. Cook the onions slowly to bring out their natural sweetness and, if possible, use homemade broth. Although some restaurants use Mozzarella cheese, the traditional preparation features Swiss or Parmesan cheese.

Yield: *6 servings*

Level: *Intermediate to challenging*

Preparation time: *15 minutes*

Cooking time: *1¼ to 1½ hours*

Freezes well (without bread and cheese)

2 tablespoons butter

2 tablespoons olive or vegetable oil

1½ pounds onions, about 4 to 5 medium, halved and thinly sliced

½ teaspoon minced fresh thyme leaves, or ¼ teaspoon dried thyme

½ teaspoon salt

¼ teaspoon freshly ground black pepper

1 tablespoon all-purpose flour

¾ cup dry white wine or vermouth (optional)

5½ cups beef or chicken broth

Additional salt to taste, about ½ teaspoon

Freshly ground black pepper to taste

6 to 12 slices lightly toasted French or Italian bread, about ½ to ¾ inch thick

1½ cups grated Gruyere or Swiss cheese, or ¾ cup freshly grated Parmesan cheese

1 In a large pot over medium heat, heat the butter and olive oil. Add the onions and sauté, stirring occasionally, until the onions are lightly golden, about 15 minutes. Reduce the heat to medium-low and continue cooking, stirring occasionally until the onions are a rich golden color, about 30 minutes. This process cannot be rushed.

2 Add the thyme, salt, and pepper and cook for 2 to 3 minutes more. Sprinkle the onions with the flour and cook, stirring almost constantly, for 1 to 2 minutes.

3 Add the wine (if desired), and cook, stirring constantly, for 1 to 2 minutes. Add the broth. Cover and simmer for 35 to 40 minutes.

4 Season with additional salt and pepper to taste.

5 Preheat the oven to 400 degrees F. Ladle the hot soup into individual ovenproof soup bowls or into an oven-proof casserole so that the soup nearly reaches the top of the container and place on a foil-lined baking sheet. Float the toasted bread on top of the hot soup and sprinkle the bread evenly with cheese. Bake until the cheese is melted, about 2 to 4 minutes, and serve immediately.

Per Serving: Calories 332.3; Protein 15.8g; Carbohydrates 25.8g; Dietary fiber 2.9g; Total fat 18.3g; Saturated fat 8.4g; Cholesterol 40.1mg; Sodium 1571.4mg.

Consommé

This French classic, a crystal-clear soup, can be served as a starter to a dinner menu. Low in calories, it is a dieter's delight.

Yield: 4 to 6 servings

Level: Intermediate to challenging

Preparation time: 45 minutes

Freezes well

1 ½ quarts homemade chicken or beef broth   Salt to taste

3 egg whites

1 In a large saucepan over medium-low heat, heat the broth until it is gently bubbling but not boiling.

2 In a medium bowl, beat the egg whites until foamy. Add the egg whites to the broth. Stir occasionally until the broth starts to bubble gently. Do not stir again. The foam from the egg whites will rise to the surface. Make a hole in the center of the foam with a spoon. Simmer until the foam becomes firmer on the surface, about 20 to 30 minutes. Remove the pot from the burner.

3 Meanwhile, line a sieve with a lightly moistened piece of cheesecloth or a clean dish towel and put it over a deep bowl or large saucepan.

4 Using a wooden spoon, carefully push the foam from the hole in the center back to the sides of the pot. Ladle the consommé out through the hole in the foam and put into the sieve and strain.

5 Reheat the strained, clear consommé, and season with salt to taste.

Caution: When ladling the soup into the sieve, make certain that the bottom of the sieve does not touch the already strained consomme or it will become cloudy again.

Variation: For another traditional presentation, add ¼ cup of finely diced vegetables, such as carrots and celery, to the consommé. Heat until the vegetables are tender, about 5 minutes.

Per Serving: Calories 37.5; Protein 2.3g; Carbohydrates 3.2g; Dietary fiber 0.8g; Total fat 1.8g; Saturated fat 0.5g; Cholesterol 1.5mg; Sodium 159.7mg.

Minestrone

Minestrone is one of Italy's most famous and beloved dishes. Vegetables, beans, and pasta join forces in this robust soup. Always serve with freshly grated Parmesan cheese.

Yield: *6 servings*

Level: *Easy*

Preparation time: *20 minutes*

Cooking time: *50 to 60 minutes*

Freezes well

3 tablespoons olive oil

1 medium onion, chopped

2 medium carrots, chopped

2 medium celery stalks, chopped

2 ounces lean ham, diced

2 plump cloves garlic, minced

7 cups chicken or vegetable broth

¼ small Savoy or green cabbage, thinly sliced, about 1¼ cups shredded

2 small zucchini or yellow squash, cut in half-moons

One 14-ounce can plum tomatoes with juice, broken into pieces with the back of a spoon

One 15- to 16-ounce can white beans (or pink or red beans), drained and rinsed

2 tablespoons chopped flat-leaf parsley

1 tablespoon chopped fresh basil, or 1 teaspoon dried basil

⅔ cup small elbow macaroni, small shells, or ditalini

Salt to taste, about ½ to ¾ teaspoon

½ teaspoon freshly ground black pepper

Freshly grated Parmesan cheese for garnish

1 In a large pot over medium-low heat, heat the olive oil. Add the onion, carrot, celery, and ham and sauté, stirring occasionally, until the onions are translucent, about 5 to 7 minutes. Add the garlic and cook, stirring often, for 2 minutes.

2 Add the broth, cabbage, zucchini, tomatoes, beans, parsley, and basil. Increase the heat to medium and bring to a boil.

3 Reduce the heat to medium-low. Simmer, partially covered, for 30 to 40 minutes.

4 Add the macaroni and simmer until the pasta is tender, about 10 to 12 minutes.

5 Taste and season with salt and pepper. Serve with Parmesan cheese on the side.

Cook's Fact: *The Italian word for soup is minestra. Minestrone literally means "big soup." There are many versions of this hearty entree, but they always include beans.*

Per Serving: *Calories 233.9; Protein 8.4g; Carbohydrates 23.7g; Dietary fiber 5.4g; Total fat 12.5g; Saturated fat 2.3g; Cholesterol 10.3mg; Sodium 1690.2mg.*

Snow Pea, Mushroom, and Scallion Soup

A wonderfully light soup with an Asian touch, this fragrant dish is scented with ginger and Chinese sesame oil.

Yield: *6 to 8 servings*

Level: *Easy*

Preparation time: *10 minutes*

Cooking time: *20 to 25 minutes*

Freezes well

7 cups homemade, unsalted chicken broth

1 tablespoon fresh lemon or lime juice

2 to 3 tablespoons soy sauce, or more to taste

6 scallions, white and green parts, sliced on an angle, with white and green parts kept separate

1 tablespoon minced ginger, about 1-inch piece

3 to 4 ounces ramen or very thin egg noodles, broken in half

½ pound shredded or cubed chicken, about 1 cup

1 tablespoon vegetable oil

6 medium shiitake (stems removed and discarded), cremini, or white mushrooms, sliced

2 ounces snow peas, trimmed and sliced in half crosswise on an angle

1½ teaspoons sesame oil

1 In a large pot over medium heat, combine the broth, lemon juice, soy sauce, white part of the scallions, ginger, ramen, and chicken. Cover and simmer 10 to 15 minutes.

2 Meanwhile, in a small skillet, heat the vegetable oil. Add the mushrooms and cook until tender, about 5 minutes. Set aside.

3 Add the mushrooms and snow peas and simmer until the snow peas are tender-crisp, about 3 minutes. Stir in the reserved scallion greens and sesame oil.

Variation: *For a vegetarian version, substitute vegetable or mushroom broth for the chicken broth. Replace the chicken with 2 ounces cubed, firm tofu, adding it with the mushrooms and snow peas.*

Per Serving: *Calories 284.0; Protein 23.6g; Carbohydrates 12.7g; Dietary fiber 1.6g; Total fat 15.1g; Saturated fat 3.7g; Cholesterol 76.5mg; Sodium 347.4mg; Notes: used egg noodles in analysis.*

Matzo Ball Soup

The homespun favorite, the pride of many Jewish grandmothers, features matzo balls and "Jewish penicillin" — otherwise known as chicken soup. Matzo balls are traditionally made with schmaltz or chicken fat, but I've lightened the recipe and used vegetable oil.

Yield: *6 to 8 servings*

Level: *Intermediate*

Preparation time: *30 minutes*

Standing time: *20 minutes to 2 hours*

Cooking time: *25 to 35 minutes*

Freezes well

For the matzo balls

2 eggs	3 tablespoons broth or water
½ teaspoon salt	1 tablespoon vegetable oil
⅛ teaspoon white pepper	⅔ cup matzo meal
Pinch ginger or cinnamon	

For the soup

6 cups chicken broth	2 tablespoons chopped fresh parsley
1 cup cooked, shredded chicken (optional)	1 tablespoon snipped fresh dill

1 **To prepare the matzo balls:** In a medium bowl, beat the eggs well. Add the salt, pepper, and ginger. Add the chicken broth and vegetable oil. Add the matzo meal and stir to blend. Cover and let stand for 20 minutes or cover and refrigerate for up to 2 hours. The dough will thicken. With wet hands, form the dough into 12 balls, using about a table-spoon of dough for each ball.

2 **To cook the matzo balls:** Drop the balls into a large pot of lightly salted, boiling water and cook for 15 to 20 minutes. Remove them with a slotted spoon and set aside until you're ready to add to them to the prepared simmering soup.

3 **To prepare the soup:** In a large pot over medium heat, combine the broth and cooked chicken (if desired) and simmer until hot. Add the matzo balls and heat thoroughly, about 10 minutes. Stir in the parsley and dill.

Tip: *Add 1 tablespoon chopped fresh parsley to the matzo ball dough to add more color to the soup.*

Per Serving: *Calories 90.7; Protein 3.2g; Carbohydrates 5.9g; Dietary fiber 0.3g; Total fat 6.1g; Saturated fat 1.3g; Cholesterol 57.0mg; Sodium 934.5mg.*

African Gingered Chicken Rice Soup

Scented with ginger, allspice, cardamom, and bay leaf, this unique soup is an outstanding variation of chicken rice soup.

Yield: *6 servings*

Level: *Easy*

Preparation time: *10 to 15 minutes*

Cooking time: *40 minutes*

Freezes well

2 tablespoons vegetable oil

1 medium onion, quartered and thinly sliced

2 tablespoons minced fresh ginger, about 2-inch piece

4 whole allspice berries or cloves

4 whole cardamom pods

1 bay leaf

8 ounces boneless chicken breast, cut into bite size cubes or very thin strips, or 1½ cups cooked shredded or cubed chicken

5½ cups chicken broth

½ cup white rice

2 tablespoons fresh lemon or lime juice

Salt to taste, about ½ to ¾ teaspoon

½ teaspoon freshly ground black pepper

⅓ cup coarsely chopped fresh cilantro

Fresh ginger, peeled and very thinly sliced into matchstick-sized strips for garnish (optional)

1 In a large pot over medium heat, heat the oil. Add the onion, ginger, allspice berries, cardamom, and bay leaf and sauté, stirring occasionally, until the onions are tender, about 10 to 12 minutes.

2 Add the chicken and cook, stirring occasionally, until the chicken turns white, about 3 to 5 minutes. If using cooked chicken, sauté for only 1 to 3 minutes.

3 Add the chicken broth and bring to a gentle boil. Add the rice. Cover partially and simmer until the rice is tender and the chicken is cooked through, about 20 minutes.

4 Add the lemon juice. Season with salt and pepper and simmer for 5 minutes. Stir in the cilantro. Garnish with additional ginger (if desired), and serve.

Tip: To bring out the most flavor, the spices need to be sautéed with the onions before they're simmered in the broth. If you want to remove the whole spices (allspice, cardamom, and bay leaf), lift them out with a skimmer or slotted spoon before serving.

Per Serving: Calories 190.1; Protein 10.9g; Carbohydrates 15.2g; Dietary fiber 0.6g; Total fat 9.3g; Saturated fat 1.5g; Cholesterol 27.0mg; Sodium 1130.4mg.

Hot and Sour Soup

This recipe is based on the famous soup native to the Szechuan province located in western China. Feel free to add extra vinegar or chili oil, according to your taste.

Yield: *6 servings*

Level: *Easy to intermediate*

Preparation time: *30 minutes*

Cooking time: *20 to 25 minutes*

Do not freeze

4 to 6 dried wood or cloud ear mushrooms

3 to 4 dried shiitake mushrooms

2½ tablespoons cornstarch

3 tablespoons water

3 tablespoons rice wine or white wine vinegar

3 tablespoons soy sauce

1 teaspoon freshly ground black pepper

4 cups chicken broth

¼ cup bamboo shoots, cut into thin, matchstick-sized strips

¼ pound boneless pork loin chop or boneless chicken breast, very thinly sliced into matchstick-sized strips

1½ teaspoons minced fresh ginger, about ½-inch piece

3 ounces firm tofu, cubed

1 large egg, beaten

1 tablespoon sesame oil

2 medium scallions, white and green parts, thinly sliced

Chinese chili oil or Tabasco to taste

1 Soak the dried mushrooms in 1½ cups boiling water for 20 minutes. Strain the liquid through a sieve lined with a paper coffee filter and reserve the liquid. Cut the mushrooms into very thin strips.

2 In a small bowl, combine the cornstarch and water and set aside.

3 In another small bowl, combine the vinegar, soy sauce, and black pepper and set aside.

4 In a large pot over medium heat, heat the broth and reserved mushroom liquid until simmering. Add the mushrooms, bamboo shoots, pork or chicken, ginger, and vinegar-soy sauce mixture and simmer for 2 to 3 minutes.

5 Stir the cornstarch mixture and add it to the pot. Bring to a boil, add the tofu, and cook for 2 to 3 minutes.

6 While stirring the soup with a fork, pour in the egg and stir until the egg has firmed into fine threads, about 1 to 2 minutes.

7 Remove from the heat immediately. Add the sesame oil and chopped scallions. Season to taste with chili oil. Add a small amount of additional vinegar if you want a more sour flavor. Serve immediately.

Tip: *To make slicing fresh meat or poultry easier, put it in the freezer for 10 to 15 minutes before slicing. The meat will be firm enough to make thin slicing an easy task.*

Per Serving: Calories 137.6; Protein 7.7g; Carbohydrates 8.3g; Dietary fiber 0.5g; Total fat 8.3g; Saturated fat 2.0g; Cholesterol 50.7mg; Sodium 1204.9mg.

Italian Chicken, Greens, and Tortellini Soup

Quick and easy, this simple and tasty soup is a wonderful addition to your repertoire.

Yield: *6 to 8 servings*

Level: *Easy*

Preparation time: *10 to 15 minutes*

Cooking time: *20 to 25 minutes*

Freezes well

2 tablespoons olive oil

5 to 6 scallions, white part only, sliced

1 red bell pepper, sliced into thin strips

3 to 4 shiitake (stems removed and discarded), cremini, or white mushrooms, sliced

1 plump clove garlic, minced

6 cups chicken broth

4 ounces cooked, shredded chicken, about ⅔ cup

2 cups thinly sliced greens such as escarole or spinach

4 ounces cheese or mushroom tortellini

Salt to taste, about ½ to ¾ teaspoon

½ teaspoon freshly ground black pepper

Freshly grated Parmesan cheese (optional)

1 In a large pot over medium heat, heat the olive oil. Add the scallions and bell pepper and sauté, stirring occasionally, about 5 minutes. Add the mushrooms and garlic and cook, stirring often, for 2 to 3 minutes.

2 Add the broth. Cover and bring to a boil. Add the chicken, greens, and tortellini. Cover partially and simmer until the greens and tortellini are tender, about 10 minutes. Season with salt and pepper. Serve with Parmesan cheese on the side (if desired).

Tip: *One of the filled pastas, tortellini, is small and doughnut-shaped. It is available frozen, dried, or fresh in the dairy case of most supermarkets. You may need to alter the cooking time slightly, depending on which type you use.*

Per Serving: Calories 150.0; Protein 8.0g; Carbohydrates 8.8g; Dietary fiber 1.2g; Total fat 9.2g; Saturated fat 2.3g; Cholesterol 19.9mg; Sodium 991.9mg.

Indonesian Shrimp Soup with Noodles

Noodle soups are a staple throughout much of Asia, including Indonesia. They can feature chicken, pork, beef, vegetables, or shrimp, as in this incredibly light version.

Yield: *4 to 6 servings*

Level: *Easy*

Preparation time: *20 minutes*

Cooking time: *20 to 25 minutes*

Do not freeze

3 cups shrimp, fish, or vegetable broth

2 tablespoons fresh lemon juice

1 tablespoon soy sauce

1 tablespoon dark brown sugar

2 plump cloves garlic, minced

1½ teaspoons minced ginger, about ½-inch piece

4 ounces ramen-style noodles or thin Chinese egg noodles

½ pound medium shrimp, peeled and deveined

2 bird's-eye chili peppers or jalapeños, seeded and thinly sliced

1 scallion, white and green parts, cut into ½-inch pieces

½ medium cucumber, peeled, seeded, and cut into very thin strips, about 1 inch long (about ¾ cup)

1 cup fresh mung bean sprouts

1 tablespoon fresh chopped mint or cilantro

1 In a large pot over medium heat, combine the broth, lemon juice, soy sauce, sugar, garlic, and ginger. Simmer for 10 to 15 minutes.

2 Add the noodles and cook until tender, about 3 to 5 minutes, or cook according to package directions.

3 Add the shrimp and the chilies to the broth and cook until the shrimp turn pink and begin to curl, about 3 minutes. Do not overcook the shrimp.

4 Remove the soup from the heat and add the scallions and cucumber.

5 To serve, ladle the soup into bowls and divide the bean sprouts equally on top. Garnish with chopped mint or cilantro.

Cook's Fact: *Bean sprouts come in several varieties: alfalfa, used in salads, and mung bean, which are often found in Chinese and Asian dishes. Mung bean sprouts are found either fresh or canned, but the canned variety lacks both crispness and flavor. If you can't find fresh for this recipe, omit them.*

Per Serving: *Calories 127.5; Protein 9.7g; Carbohydrates 18.6g; Dietary fiber 1.3g; Total fat 1.9g; Saturated fat 0.6g; Cholesterol 62.0mg; Sodium 287.6mg.*

Mulligatawny Soup

Several versions of Mulligatawny exist, some with lentils, and some with chicken. This one is a lightly curried chicken soup that hails from southern India. Here, grated apples add texture and balance the spiciness of the curry. It's your choice whether to use coconut milk or cream, but always serve the soup over rice.

Yield: *6 to 8 servings*

Level: *Easy*

Preparation time: *15 minutes*

Cooking time: *40 to 45 minutes*

Freezes well (leave out the coconut milk if freezing, and add to thawed soup when reheating)

2 tablespoons vegetable oil

1 medium onion, chopped

2 plump cloves garlic, minced

1 tablespoon minced ginger, about 1-inch piece

1 to 2 tablespoons good quality curry powder, preferably Madras

¾ pound boneless chicken breasts or thighs, cut into bite-sized cubes

2 medium sweet apples, such as Golden Delicious or Cortland, peeled and coarsely grated, about 1¾ cups

3 to 4 cups chicken broth

¾ to 1 cup unsweetened coconut milk, half-and-half, or cream (optional)

Salt to taste, about ½ teaspoon

1 cup cooked rice

1 In a large pot over medium heat, heat the vegetable oil. Add the onion and sauté, stirring occasionally, until translucent, about 5 minutes. Add the garlic, ginger, and curry powder and cook, stirring constantly, for 1 to 2 minutes.

2 Add the chicken and cook, stirring occasionally, until the chicken turns white, about 5 minutes. Add the apples and 3 cups of the broth (or 4 cups if not using the coconut milk or half-and-half).

3 Reduce the heat to medium-low. Cover and simmer until the chicken is cooked and the apples are very tender and partially disintegrated, about 25 to 30 minutes. Add the coconut milk (if desired) and salt and heat thoroughly, about 5 minutes.

4 Put a tablespoon or two of cooked rice into each bowl and ladle the soup over the rice.

Cook's Fact: *Curry powder is not a spice, but a blend of several spices ground into a fine powder. Typically, it includes cardamom, cinnamon, chilies, cloves, coriander, cumin, fennel seeds, ground red pepper, black pepper, and turmeric, although a range of other spices may also be added.*

Per Serving: *Calories 146.5; Protein 10.7g; Carbohydrates 12.0g; Dietary fiber 1.2g; Total fat 6.2g; Saturated fat 0.9g; Cholesterol 27.1mg; Sodium 541.7mg.*

Bread Soup

Made with fresh tomatoes and stale bread, versions of this soup are found in Italy, most notably Tuscany and Calabria-Lucania.

Although it can also be successfully prepared with canned tomatoes, ripe fresh tomatoes are best! This soup can be served hot or, my preference, at room temperature.

An alternative way of serving this soup is to put the torn bread into each bowl and ladle the soup on top.

Yield: *6 servings*

Level: *Easy*

Preparation time: *15 to 20 minutes*

Cooking time: *30 to 35 minutes*

Standing time (if serving at room temperature): *45 to 60 minutes*

Do not freeze

3 tablespoons extra virgin olive oil	*2½ cups chicken or vegetable broth*
1 small onion, chopped	*½ bay leaf*
1 celery stalk, chopped	*Salt to taste, about ½ to 1 teaspoon*
2 to 3 plump cloves garlic, minced	*¼ teaspoon freshly ground black pepper*
¼ teaspoon crushed red chili flakes, or ½ jalapeño, seeded and minced	*4 to 6 slices stale Italian bread or fresh Italian bread lightly toasted*
1½ pounds ripe tomatoes, peeled, seeded, and coarsely chopped, or one 28-ounce can Italian plum tomatoes, drained and coarsely chopped or broken with the back of a wooden spoon	*1½ tablespoons chopped fresh basil*
	Freshly grated Romano or Parmesan cheese

1 In a large pot over medium heat, heat the olive oil. Add the onion and celery and sauté, stirring occasionally, until almost tender, about 10 minutes. Add the garlic and chili flakes and cook, stirring constantly, for 1 minute.

2 Add the tomatoes and cook, stirring occasionally, for 7 to 10 minutes.

3 Add the broth and bay leaf and simmer for 10 to 15 minutes. Season with salt to taste and black pepper.

4 Tear the bread into small pieces and add to the soup. Let stand for 2 to 3 minutes. Stir in the basil. Serve with Romano cheese on the side. Serve hot or at room temperature. If serving at room temperature, let stand until cooled, about 45 to 60 minutes.

Per Serving: *Calories 159.9; Protein 3.4g; Carbohydrates 16.6g; Dietary fiber 2.1g; Total fat 9.5g; Saturated fat 1.6g; Cholesterol 2.1mg; Sodium 744.6mg.*

Sicilian Fish Soup

Like many Mediterranean fish soups, this one uses a combination of seafood: white fish filets and scallops. The broth is enhanced with herbs, orange zest, and chili flakes.

Yield: *4 to 6 servings*

Level: *Easy*

Preparation time: *10 to 15 minutes*

Cooking time: *30 to 35 minutes*

Do not freeze

2 tablespoons olive oil

1 medium onion, chopped

1 celery stalk, chopped

2 to 3 plump cloves garlic, chopped

3½ cups fish or vegetable broth, or 1½ cups clam juice and 2 cups water

½ cup dry white wine or vermouth

1½ cups chopped canned tomatoes, or 3 medium fresh tomatoes, peeled and seeded

2-inch strip orange or lemon zest

1 teaspoon minced fresh thyme leaves, or ½ teaspoon dried thyme

½ bay leaf

¼ teaspoon red chili flakes (optional)

1 pound combination of fish filets, such as cod, grouper, tilefish, scrod, monkfish, snapper, or other firm textured white fish cut into 1½-inch strips or chunks

½ pound sea scallops, or an additional ½ pound of fish

3 tablespoons chopped fresh flat-leaf parsley

3 to 4 slices Italian bread, lightly toasted

1 In a large pot over medium heat, heat the olive oil. Add the onion and celery and cook, stirring occasionally, about 5 to 7 minutes. Add the garlic and cook, stirring often, for 1 minute.

2 Add the fish broth, wine, tomatoes, orange zest, thyme, bay leaf, and chili flakes (if desired). Cover and simmer for 15 minutes.

3 Add the fish and scallops and simmer, uncovered, until the fish is cooked through, about 10 minutes.

4 Stir in the parsley. To serve, tear the bread in pieces and put into soup bowls. Ladle the soup on top.

Variation: *Add a few cleaned clams or mussels when you add the fish, but discard any that have not opened.*

Per Serving: *Calories 241.0; Protein 21.5g; Carbohydrates 23.5g; Dietary fiber 3.5g; Total fat 6.5g; Saturated fat 1.0g; Cholesterol 36.8mg; Sodium 334.9mg.*

Hearty Winter Borscht

Borscht is a soup from Russia, the Ukraine, and Poland, with many variations. Some are hot and some are cold, but they all contain beets. This robust version combines beets, cabbage, and beef, and should always be served hot.

Yield: *6 to 8 servings*

Level: *Easy*

Preparation time: *15 minutes*

Cooking time: *1¼ to 1½ hours*

Freezes well

1 pound beef chuck, cut into ½-inch cubes

6 cups beef broth or water

¾ pound beets

1 medium onion, thinly sliced

1 medium carrot, finely diced

1½ cups shredded cabbage

One 14-ounce can chopped tomatoes, drained

1 bay leaf

2 tablespoons white wine vinegar or fresh lemon juice

2 teaspoons sugar

Salt to taste, about ½ teaspoon

½ teaspoon freshly ground black pepper

Sour cream for garnish

Snipped fresh dill for garnish (optional)

1 In a large pot over medium heat, combine the beef and water, cover partially, and simmer until the meat is almost tender, about 35 to 40 minutes.

2 Meanwhile, put the beets in a medium saucepan and cover with plenty of cold water. Boil the beets until tender and drain in a colander. When the beets are cool enough to handle, peel and cut them into bite-sized wedges and set aside.

3 Add the onion, carrot, cabbage, tomatoes, and bay leaf to the pot. Simmer, covered, until the vegetables and meat are very tender, about 30 to 35 minutes longer.

4 Add the beets, vinegar, and sugar and simmer, partially covered, for 15 to 20 minutes. Serve garnished with a dollop of sour cream and dill (if desired).

Cook's Fact: *Vinegar is derived from the French words* vin aigre *which literally means "sour wine." Some vinegars, particularly distilled white vinegar, are very acidic and bitter. Wine vinegars, however, have a pleasingly tart aroma and taste.*

Per Serving: *Calories 186.1; Protein 14.9g; Carbohydrates 8.0g; Dietary fiber 2.0g; Total fat 10.2g; Saturated fat 4.0g; Cholesterol 38.7mg; Sodium 1027.4mg.*

Curried Mussel Soup

Mussels accented with a touch of Indian curry are superb, especially in this chunky soup full of tomatoes and potatoes.

Remove freshly cooked mussels from their shells for this soup. If the mussels are large, as "farm raised" or "cultivated" ones sometimes are, cut them in half. Using fresh mussels is best and for an exotic and colorful look; try New Zealand mussels that have a greenish-black shell (which we used in the photo of the soup). These, like several other varieties, are available frozen. Occasionally, fishmongers will sell freshly cooked mussels out of the shell. Sometimes, you'll also find them frozen or canned.

Yield: *6 servings*

Level: *Easy (intermediate if using fresh mussels)*

Preparation time: *10 to 15 minutes if using canned mussels, 45 to 60 minutes if using fresh mussels*

Cooking time: *40 to 45 minutes*

Do not freeze

2 tablespoons vegetable oil

1 small onion, thinly sliced

1 medium carrot, finely diced

2 plump cloves garlic, minced

2 to 3 teaspoons good quality curry powder, preferably Madras

1 cup canned chopped tomatoes, or 2 medium tomatoes, peeled, seeded, and chopped

1 medium potato, finely diced

3 cups fish broth, or 1 cup clam juice and 2 cups water

3 to 3½ dozen cooked fresh mussels, or two 3½-ounce cans, drained, with juice reserved for broth

Salt to taste, about ½ to ¾ teaspoon

Freshly chopped cilantro or parsley for garnish

1 In a large pot over medium heat, heat the vegetable oil. Add the onion and carrot and sauté until the onion is lightly golden, about 10 to 15 minutes. Add the garlic and curry powder and cook, stirring constantly, for 2 minutes.

2 Add the tomatoes and cook, stirring for 2 minutes. Add the potato and broth. Cover and simmer until the potato is tender, about 20 minutes.

3 Add the mussels and salt and simmer until heated through, about 3 to 5 minutes. Garnish with chopped cilantro.

Per Serving: *Calories 207.0; Protein 13.7g; Carbohydrates 22.1g; Dietary fiber 3.2g; Total fat 7.0g; Saturated fat 0.8g; Cholesterol 26.9mg; Sodium 588.7mg.*

Thai Coconut Chicken Soup

This velvety smooth and delicately flavored soup with hint of chilies creates the perfect contrast of spicy and sweet. Add an extra chili if you want the authentic burn of Thai food.

Yield: *6 servings*

Level: *Easy*

Preparation time: *10 minutes*

Cooking time: *20 to 25 minutes*

Do not freeze

2½ cups chicken broth

2 cups unsweetened coconut milk

2 tablespoons Thai fish sauce or soy sauce

2 Thai or kaffir lime leaves (optional)

1 fresh stalk lemon grass, chopped, or 2 tablespoons dried, or 1 teaspoon grated fresh lemon zest

1 teaspoon fresh minced ginger, about ¼-inch piece

2 bird's-eye chili peppers, or 1 to 2 jalapeños seeded and minced

12 ounces boneless chicken breasts

2 tablespoons fresh lime juice

1 teaspoon sugar

¼ cup cilantro leaves, whole or minced

1 In a large pot over medium heat, combine the chicken broth, coconut milk, fish sauce, lime leaves (if desired), lemon grass, ginger, and chilies. Bring to a boil.

2 Reduce the heat to medium-low. Add the chicken and simmer for 10 to 15 minutes or until the chicken is cooked through.

3 Add the lime juice and sugar and simmer for 3 to 5 minutes. Float the cilantro leaves on top or garnish with chopped cilantro.

Cook's Fact: *Cilantro, a leafy herb that looks similar to flat-leaf parsley, is used in southeast Asian and Mexican cooking. Also called Chinese parsley or coriander, it is actually the leaf of the coriander plant, the seeds of which are dried and ground and used as a spice.*

Per Serving: *Calories 100.3; Protein 13.7g; Carbohydrates 3.3g; Dietary fiber 0.1g; Total fat 3.4g; Saturated fat 0.8g; Cholesterol 35.7mg; Sodium 946.1mg.*

Japanese Vegetable and Pork Soup

This uncomplicated soup highlighted with ginger is quick to prepare and very good.

Yield: *4 to 6 servings*

Level: *Easy*

Preparation time: *10 minutes*

Cooking time: *25 to 35 minutes*

Do not freeze

1½ tablespoons vegetable oil

¼ pound ground lean pork or chicken

2-inch piece daikon, quartered and cut into very thin strips, or 5 medium radishes, sliced and cut into thin strips

2-inch piece carrot, quartered and cut into very thin strips

4½ cups dashi (see Chapter 5) or chicken broth

1 to 2 tablespoons soy sauce

3 to 4 shiitake (stems removed and discarded) or white mushrooms, sliced

2 ounces firm tofu, cubed

1 scallion, white and green parts, cut into ½-inch pieces

2 tablespoons grated fresh ginger, about 1½- to 2-inch piece

1 In a large pot over medium heat, heat the vegetable oil. Add the pork and cook, stirring occasionally and breaking up any lumps, until the pork is cooked through, about 7 minutes. Add the daikon and carrot and stir-fry for 3 minutes.

2 Add the dashi and season with soy sauce. The amount you use will depend on the saltiness of the broth itself, so taste it beforehand. Simmer for 5 minutes.

3 Add the mushrooms and tofu and cook until the mushrooms are tender, about 3 to 5 minutes. Do not let the soup boil.

4 Add the scallion and remove the soup from the heat.

5 Wrap the grated ginger in a piece of cheesecloth. Hold the cloth over the soup and wring gently to squeeze the ginger juice into the soup. Serve immediately.

Cook's Fact: *Daikon, a long white root with a sweet flavor and crisp texture, is used in Japanese cooking. It is a wonderful addition to soups, salads, and stir-fries.*

Per Serving: *Calories 113; Protein 7.4g; Carbohydrates 3.8g; Dietary fiber 0.5g; Total fat 7.7g; Saturated fat 1.5g; Cholesterol 18.4mg; Sodium 534.9mg.*

Miso and Vegetable Soup

Miso, a mainstay of the Japanese diet, is made from fermented soybean paste and is often used in soups. In Japan, some miso soups are eaten for breakfast, but feel free to eat this one for a surprisingly quick lunch, dinner, or snack.

Yield: *4 to 6 servings*

Level: *Easy*

Preparation time: *15 to 20 minutes*

Do not freeze

4 cups dashi (see Chapter 5) or chicken broth

1 teaspoon soy sauce

2 tablespoons sake or rice wine (optional)

2-inch piece daikon, quartered and sliced into thin strips

3-inch piece carrot, halved and sliced into thin strips

3 green beans, cut into 1-inch pieces

3 tablespoons light or red miso, or a combination of the two

2 ounces firm tofu, cubed (optional)

1 scallion, white and green parts, cut into ½-inch pieces

1 In a large pot over medium heat, bring the dashi, soy sauce, and sake (if desired) to a gentle simmer. Add the daikon, carrot, and green beans and simmer until tender-crisp, about 3 to 5 minutes.

2 In a small bowl, combine the miso with ⅓ cup of the simmering broth and stir to dissolve the miso completely.

3 Add the miso mixture to the pot gradually, making sure to crush any lumps. Add the tofu. Let the soup heat thoroughly, but don't let it boil or the flavor of the miso will be ruined. Add the scallions and serve immediately.

Cook's Fact: *Miso comes in several varieties: barley miso, rice miso, and soy miso. It also comes in a variety of colors from light golden to reddish to a rich brown. High in protein and B vitamins, it also has a high sodium content. Refrigerate any unused miso in an airtight container.*

Per Serving: *Calories 40.6; Protein 3.4g; Carbohydrates 3.7g; Dietary fiber 0.6g; Total fat 1.4g; Saturated fat 0.1g; Cholesterol 5.1mg; Sodium 750.1mg.*

Chapter 15

Chill Out

*W*ho doesn't need to chill out in the summer heat? Fabulous warm weather fare, cold soups are the perfect light meal when the mercury rises. Pair them with bread or crackers and salad or use them as a starter followed by a piece of grilled chicken or fish. Fruit soups can be served either as a light lunch, as a first course in summer, or as an unusual dessert year-round.

Simple and quick to prepare, the only trick is to refrigerate them long enough so that they're icy cold. All the recipes in this chapter can be made several hours or up to a day ahead. For your convenience, I've noted in the chapter recipe list, a few soups from other chapters that also are delicious when served cold.

A few chilling clues

Take the following advice to heart when making cold soups:

- Chill cooked soups down as indicated in Chapter 4 before refrigerating them.

- Make the soup up to a day ahead so you have enough time to chill it adequately. If you are short on time, you can put cooled soup in the freezer to speed up the process and transfer it to the refrigerator after it's cold, but don't let it freeze.

- For an especially nice presentation, refrigerate individual soup bowls and serving tureens so that they're cold and the soup stays as cool as possible when you serve it.

- Sometimes soups get thicker after they are chilled. Thin those that have become a bit too thick with a splash of the same liquid that's used in the recipe: ice cold broth, milk, or juice.

Cucumber Soup

This is one of the most refreshing soups on a hot summer day.

Yield: *6 servings*

Level: *Easy*

Tools: *Food processor or blender*

Preparation time: *15 minutes*

Chilling time: *1½ to 2 hours*

Do not freeze

2 English cucumbers, unpeeled, seeded, and coarsely chopped

6 scallions, white part only, thinly sliced

3 cups buttermilk

1 cup plain yogurt

Juice of 1 lemon

1 plump clove garlic, finely minced or pressed

1½ tablespoons fresh dill or mint, minced

Salt to taste, about ½ teaspoon

¼ teaspoon white pepper

1 In a food processor or blender, combine the cucumbers and scallions and puree until smooth.

2 Add the buttermilk, yogurt, lemon juice, garlic, dill, salt, and pepper to the food processor or blender. Pulse until thoroughly mixed.

3 Chill thoroughly. Garnish with extra dill.

Tip: *To remove the seeds from a cucumber easily, slice the cucumber in half width-wise, and then in half lengthwise. Scoop the seeds out with the metal handle of a vegetable peeler, a small melon baller, or a teaspoon.*

Per Serving: *Calories 88.1; Protein 6.8g; Carbohydrates 11.7g; Dietary fiber 0.7g; Total fat 1.8g; Saturated fat 1.1g; Cholesterol 6.8mg; Sodium 353.4mg.*

Avocado Soup

Versions of this soup can be found from California to the Caribbean, Mexico, and southern Africa. Make sure that you use very ripe avocados in this buttery-textured soup.

Yield: *6 servings*

Level: *Easy*

Tools: *Food processor or blender*

Preparation time: *15 minutes*

Chilling time: *1½ to 2 hours*

Do not freeze

2 ripe medium avocados, peeled, pit removed

1 tablespoon fresh lemon juice

1 small cucumber, peeled, seeded, and cubed

1 plump clove garlic, finely minced

2 tablespoons minced fresh basil or finely chopped chives

2¼ cups chicken broth, chilled

⅔ cup plain yogurt or sour cream

Salt to taste, about ½ teaspoon

1 Cube the avocado, put the pulp in a bowl, and toss with the lemon juice.

2 In a food processor, combine the avocado, cucumber, garlic, and basil and puree until smooth.

3 Add the chicken broth and yogurt and pulse until blended.

4 Season with salt. Chill thoroughly.

Tip: *To prevent avocado flesh from discoloring after you cut it, immediately sprinkle it evenly with a little lemon juice. If the avocado is sliced or cubed, toss gently.*

Per Serving: *Calories 145.0; Protein 3.4g; Carbohydrates 8.0g; Dietary fiber 3.6g; Total fat 12.2g; Saturated fat 2.3g; Cholesterol 3.5mg; Sodium 595.0mg.*

Watercress or Swiss Chard Soup

Watercress has a slightly bitter, peppery bite. Swiss chard is a milder green with a slightly bittersweet taste that is reminiscent of spinach and beets. Both work equally well in this recipe.

To store fresh watercress, put the stems in a glass of water, cover with a plastic bag, and refrigerate for up to 3 days. To store Swiss chard, keep it in a plastic bag in the refrigerator for up to 3 days. Wash and remove any tough stems before using.

Yield: *4 to 6 servings*

Level: *Easy*

Tools: *Food processor, blender, or hand blender*

Preparation time: *25 minutes*

Chilling time: *1½ to 2 hours*

Do not freeze

2 tablespoons butter, margarine, or vegetable oil

4 medium leeks, white part only, thinly sliced, or 1 small onion, chopped

3 cups chicken or vegetable broth

1 medium potato, peeled and very thinly sliced, about 1⅓ cups

½ bay leaf

1 medium bunch watercress, stems removed, or 3 cups Swiss chard, coarse stems removed, shredded

Salt to taste, about ½ teaspoon

½ teaspoon black pepper

1⅓ cups plain yogurt

1 In a large pot over medium-low heat, melt the butter. Add the leeks and sauté, stirring occasionally, until softened, about 5 to 7 minutes.

2 Add the chicken broth, potato, and bay leaf. Increase the heat to medium, cover, and bring to a boil.

3 Add the watercress or Swiss chard, and simmer, covered, until the potato and watercress are tender, about 10 minutes.

4 Cool the soup slightly. Remove the bay leaf. Puree the mixture in batches in a blender or food processor. Alternatively, if you have a hand blender, leave the mixture in the pot and blend.

5 Transfer the puree to a bowl. Taste and season with salt and pepper. Do not add any salt if using Swiss chard. Cool the soup to lukewarm.

6 Stir in the yogurt and chill thoroughly, about 1½ to 2 hours.

Per Serving: Calories 119.9; Protein 4.2g; Carbohydrates 11.1g; Dietary fiber 0.8g; Total fat 6.8g; Saturated fat 3.4g; Cholesterol 16.2mg; Sodium 738.6mg.

Vichyssoise

Some restaurants serve this classic soup in a bowl set over a slightly larger bowl of crushed ice. Serve it well chilled and always garnish it with chopped chives.

Yield: *6 servings*

Level: *Easy*

Tools: *Food processor, blender, or hand blender*

Preparation time: *50 to 60 minutes*

Chilling time: *2 to 3 hours*

Do not freeze

2 tablespoons butter	*Salt to taste, about ½ to ¾ teaspoon*
4 medium leeks, white part only, thinly sliced	*⅛ teaspoon white pepper*
1 small onion, thinly sliced	*1¼ to 1½ cups cream or half-and-half*
3 cups chicken broth	*Chopped chives for garnish*
1½ pounds potatoes, about 3 medium, peeled and thinly sliced	

1 In a large pot over medium-low heat, melt the butter. Add the leeks and onion and sauté, stirring occasionally, until lightly golden, about 10 to 15 minutes.

2 Add the broth and potatoes. Increase the heat to medium and bring to a boil. Simmer, partially covered, until the potatoes are tender, about 25 to 30 minutes.

3 Puree in batches in a food processor or blender until smooth. Alternatively, if you have a hand blender, leave the soup in the pot and blend.

4 Transfer the soup to a large bowl. Add salt to taste and pepper. Thin with cream and stir to blend.

5 Chill thoroughly, at least 2 hours. Serve garnished with chopped chives.

Cook's Fact: *The ultimate potato soup, Vichyssoise (pronounced vee-shee-swahz), was the creation of a French chef, Louis Diat, at New York's Ritz-Carlton Hotel in the early 1900s.*

Per Serving: *Calories 325.0; Protein 3.6g; Carbohydrates 24.7g; Dietary fiber 2.3g; Total fat 24.3g; Saturated fat 14.3g; Cholesterol 80.8mg; Sodium 721.4mg.*

Cooking with mint

When recipes call for fresh mint, they usually mean spearmint. Mint comes in several varieties, including peppermint and wintergreen (whose flavor is too strong for most savory recipes). Peppermint, however, is sometimes used for ice cream, candies, and other sweets.

Lemony Minted Green Pea Soup

In the dog days of summer, this marvelous, fresh-tasting soup is superb. In cooler weather, it can also be served hot.

Yield: 6 servings

Level: Easy

Tools: Blender or hand blender

Preparation time: 25 to 30 minutes

Chilling time: 1½ to 2 hours

Freezes well

2 tablespoons butter or margarine	1 teaspoon finely grated lemon zest
1 medium onion, chopped	1¼ cups half-and-half or cream
1 plump clove garlic, minced	Salt to taste, about ½ teaspoon
3 cups chicken broth	¼ teaspoon black pepper
3¾ cups fresh or frozen peas	Fresh mint sprigs for garnish (optional)
1 cup fresh mint leaves, minced (about ¼ cup when minced)	

1 In a large pot over medium heat, melt the butter. Add the onion and sauté, stirring occasionally, until lightly golden, about 10 to 15 minutes. Add the garlic and cook, stirring occasionally, for 2 minutes.

2 Add the chicken broth and peas and bring to a boil. Reduce the heat to medium-low and simmer for 5 to 10 minutes until the peas are cooked. Add the mint leaves and cook for 2 minutes.

3 Strain the solids, reserving the broth. In a blender, puree the peas in batches with a small amount of broth until smooth. Alternatively, if you have a hand blender, remove and reserve ½ cup of broth and blend the remaining mixture in the pot.

4 In a large bowl, combine the pureed peas, lemon zest, and half-and-half and stir in enough of the reserved broth, about 2 cups, to make the desired consistency. If you have used a hand blender, transfer the pureed pea and broth mixture to a bowl, add the lemon zest and half-and-half. Thin with the remaining ½ cup of broth if the soup is too thick. Season with salt and pepper.

5 Chill thoroughly, about 2 hours. Garnish with mint leaves (if desired).

Caution: Although this soup can be made with a food processor, it is smoother when pureed in a blender or with a hand blender or an old-fashioned food mill.

Per Serving: Calories 205.9; Protein 7.6g; Carbohydrates 18.0g; Dietary fiber 3.2g; Total fat 12.1g; Saturated fat 6.5g; Cholesterol 31.5mg; Sodium 724.0mg.

Cantaloupe-Orange Soup

Good for brunch, lunch, dinner, or dessert, this light soup can be made in a flash.

Yield: 6 to 8 servings

Level: Easy

Tools: Food processor or blender

Preparation time: 10 minutes

Chilling time: 1½ to 2 hours

Do not freeze

3 medium or 2 large very ripe cantaloupes, peeled, seeded, and cut into chunks

1¼ cups chilled fresh orange juice

Juice of 1 medium lemon or lime

¼ to ⅓ cup sherry or additional orange juice

Finely grated zest of one small orange

2 to 3 tablespoons sugar (optional)

½ teaspoon ground coriander

Pinch of salt

3 tablespoons chopped fresh mint

1 In a food processor or blender, puree the cantaloupe. Add the orange juice, lemon juice, and sherry. Pulse until smooth.

2 Transfer the soup to a bowl. Stir in the orange zest, sugar (if desired), coriander, and salt. Thin with additional orange juice if necessary. Chill thoroughly, about 1½ hours. Stir in the mint right before serving.

Tip: If you're planning to make this soup, refrigerate the melon overnight. Chilling time will be cut in half, but it will still be long enough to allow the flavors blend fully.

Per Serving: Calories 99.2; Protein 1.8g; Carbohydrates 22.7g; Dietary fiber 1.6g; Total fat 0.1g; Saturated fat 0.0g; Cholesterol 0mg; Sodium 56.0mg.

Spanish Gazpacho

Gazpacho, the quintessential summer soup from the Andalusia area of southern Spain, has many versions. This splendid rendition is tangy and slightly chunky.

Yield: *6 servings*

Level: *Easy*

Tools: *Food processor*

Preparation time: *20 minutes*

Chilling time: *1½ to 2 hours*

Do not freeze

5 ripe tomatoes, peeled, seeded, and coarsely chopped

1 medium cucumber, peeled, seeded, and coarsely chopped

1 medium green bell pepper, seeded and coarsely chopped

5 scallions, white and green parts, thinly sliced

1 to 2 jalapeño peppers, seeded and finely minced

2 plump cloves garlic, minced

3 tablespoons minced flat-leaf parsley

1½ tablespoons minced fresh basil, cilantro, or mint

1½ cups tomato juice

3 tablespoons red wine vinegar

3 tablespoons extra-virgin olive oil

Salt to taste, about 1 to 1½ teaspoons

Homemade croutons or croutes for garnish (optional)

1 In a large bowl, combine tomatoes, cucumber, bell pepper, scallions, jalapeño, garlic, parsley, and basil.

2 Put half of the vegetable mixture in a food processor and pulse several times until it forms a coarse puree. Set aside.

3 In a large liquid measuring cup, combine the tomato juice, vinegar, olive oil, and salt. Pour into the bowl with the solid vegetables. Return the pureed vegetables to the bowl and stir to mix.

4 Chill thoroughly, about 2 hours. Serve garnished with croutons or with croutes on the side (if desired).

Tip: *To reduce the chilling time, refrigerate the tomato juice and vegetables ahead of time.*

Per Serving: *Calories 122.4; Protein 2.7g; Carbohydrates 13.7g; Dietary fiber 3.0g; Total fat 7.4g; Saturated fat 1.0g; Cholesterol 0mg; Sodium 812.7mg.*

Carrot-Ginger Soup

Chock-full of ginger flavor, this zesty soup has been one of my favorites for years. It's terrific cold, but it's equally delightful when served piping hot.

Yield: *6 servings*

Level: *Easy*

Tools: *Food processor, blender, or hand blender*

Preparation time: *10 to 15 minutes*

Cooking time: *45 to 50 minutes*

Chilling time: *2 to 3 hours*

Freezes well

2 tablespoons butter or margarine	*5 cups chicken broth*
1 medium onion, chopped	*1½ pounds carrots, peeled and coarsely chopped*
1½ tablespoons minced ginger, about 1- to 1½-inch piece	*Salt to taste, about ½ teaspoon*
¼ teaspoon ground coriander, or ⅛ teaspoon ground nutmeg	*Chopped fresh cilantro for garnish*

1 In a large pot over medium heat, melt the butter. Add the onion and ginger and sauté, stirring occasionally, until almost tender, about 7 minutes. Add the coriander and cook, stirring occasionally, for 1 minute.

2 Add the chicken broth and carrots and bring to a boil. Cover partially and cook until the carrots are tender, about 35 to 40 minutes.

3 Strain, reserving the broth. Puree the vegetables with a small amount of the broth in batches in a food processor or blender until very smooth. Alternatively, if you have a hand blender, leave the soup in the pot and blend.

4 In a large bowl, combine the pureed vegetables with the broth. Season with salt. Chill thoroughly, at least 2 hours. Thin if desired with additional chilled broth or with milk or half-and-half. Serve garnished with chopped fresh cilantro.

Variation: *For a richer taste, thin this soup with ⅓ to ½ cup of cream, or to add a southeast Asian flair, use unsweetened, canned coconut milk. Do not freeze if using coconut milk.*

Per Serving: *Calories 124.4; Protein 2.5g; Carbohydrates 13.0g; Dietary fiber 3.2g; Total fat 7.2g; Saturated fat 3.2g; Cholesterol 14.5mg; Sodium 1085.6mg.*

Cold Sorrel or Spinach Soup

Readily available in spring, sorrel — a leafy green with a somewhat tart and sour taste — is delicious when mellowed in a creamy soup. If it's out of season, substitute spinach and add a tablespoon of fresh lemon juice.

Yield: *6 servings*

Level: *Easy*

Tools: *Food processor, blender, or hand blender*

Preparation time: *30 to 35 minutes*

Chilling time: *2 to 3 hours*

Do not freeze

2 tablespoons butter

5 scallions, white part only, sliced

1 medium potato, peeled and cut into ½-inch chunks

4 cups chicken or vegetable broth

1 pound sorrel, washed and coarsely chopped

¼ teaspoon white pepper

Salt to taste, about ½ teaspoon

1 cup cream, sour cream, or nonfat sour cream

Snipped fresh dill or chopped chives for garnish

1 In a large pot over medium heat, melt the butter. Add the scallions and sauté, stirring occasionally, until tender, about 5 minutes. Add the potatoes and cook, stirring occasionally, for 5 minutes.

2 Add the broth and sorrel and bring to a boil. Cook until the potatoes and sorrel are tender, about 15 to 20 minutes.

3 Puree in batches in a blender or food processor until smooth. Alternatively, if you have a hand blender, leave the soup in the pot and blend.

4 Transfer to a bowl and add the pepper and salt. Chill thoroughly, at least 2 hours.

5 Before serving, stir in the cream, and garnish with fresh dill.

Cook's Fact: *Leafy greens, such as sorrel, Swiss chard, and spinach, are an excellent source of Vitamins A and C and are rich in iron.*

Per Serving: *Calories 232.5; Protein 3.1g; Carbohydrates 8.3g; Dietary fiber 2.1g; Total fat 21.6g; Saturated fat 12.2g; Cholesterol 68.1mg; Sodium 879.4mg.*

Very Berry Fruit Gazpacho

A combination of berries creates this delectable, fragrantly spiced fruit soup. It's a cooling and refreshing soup indeed!

Wrap the whole spices in cheesecloth to form a *bouquet garni* that can be removed easily from the soup before pureeing.

Yield: 4 to 6 servings

Level: Easy to intermediate

Tools: Food processor, blender, or hand blender

Preparation time: 20 to 25 minutes

Chilling time: 2 to 3 hours

Freezes well without diced fruit

4 to 5 cups mixed unsweetened frozen or fresh berries, such as blueberries, blackberries, sliced strawberries, raspberries, or pitted cherries

2 cups water

½ cup ruby port or red wine (optional)

⅔ to 1 cup sugar, or to taste

2 allspice berries or whole cloves

1 cinnamon stick

1 small, quarter-sized slice of fresh ginger

1½ cups diced fruit, such as kiwi, pineapple, mango, papaya, or strawberries (optional)

Mint leaves for garnish

Whipped cream or yogurt for garnish (optional)

1 In a large pot over medium heat, combine the berries, water, port (if desired), sugar, allspice, cinnamon, and ginger. Cover and bring to a boil. Reduce the heat to medium-low and simmer, uncovered, until the berries are very soft, about 10 to 15 minutes. Taste for sugar, adding more if you want.

2 With a slotted spoon, remove the whole spices and ginger. Puree the mixture in batches in a food processor or blender until smooth. Alternatively, if you have a hand blender, leave the soup in the pot and blend.

3 Strain through a fine mesh sieve into a clean bowl to remove seeds, pressing lightly on the sieve with the back of a spoon.

4 Chill thoroughly, at least 2 hours.

5 To serve, divide the diced fruit (if desired) among bowls and ladle the soup on top. Garnish with mint leaves and a dollop of whipped cream or yogurt (if desired).

Cook's Fact: *Usually more tart than overly sweet, fruit soups are typical of Scandinavian fare. Recipes were brought by immigrants to the United States. Although they are most often served cold, they can also be served hot.*

Per Serving: Calories 145.0; Protein 0.6g; Carbohydrates 37.0g; Dietary fiber 3.3g; Total fat 0.4g; Saturated fat 0.0g; Cholesterol 0mg; Sodium 5.0mg.

Part V

From the Ladle to the Table

The 5th Wave   By Rich Tennant

"Oh, I have a very healthy relationship with food. It's the relationship I have with my scale that's not so good."

In this part . . .

Getting food on the table takes some advance preparation. Serving is easiest if you decide beforehand where you're going to eat (kitchen, den, dining room or patio) and how (on a TV tray, at the dining table or breakfast bar). Set the table and assemble whatever bowls, underplates, utensils, such as spoons and ladles, and any other serving pieces you might need. Are the soup bowls warmed? Are you having bread? Do you want to warm it and put it in a basket? Are you making a salad? Are the salad plates chilled; is the dressing made? This part helps you to have all of these items in place so that when it's time to sit down, you don't have to rush to finish last-minute details.

Chapter 16

It's Your Serve

W hether you're planning a casual supper or a formal dinner, presentation sets the tone. Consider what accompaniments will round out the menu and what garnishes you will use. These extra touches do make a difference.

Serving Hot Soups

Nothing is more comforting than a hot bowl of soup. The trick is to keep it that way. When serving hot soup, warm the bowls. One way is to heat them in a preheated oven at a low temperature (200 to 250 degrees F) for a few minutes. If your oven is being used for something else, pour boiling water from a kettle into the bowls and let them stand for several minutes. Pour out the water, dry the bowls, and ladle in the piping hot soup immediately.

Serving Chilled Soups

In summer, cold soups are refreshingly delightful. Chill the bowls in the refrigerator for an hour or more. Don't put them in the freezer unless they're freezer-proof, or they can crack.

Warming tureens

Tureens or large serving bowls should be heated or chilled, as necessary. The easiest way to heat tureens is with boiling water. Place the tureen on a trivet or underplate so that it doesn't leave a permanent mark on a wooden table. Some stainless and enameled cooking pots are pretty enough for serving on the sideboard and retain heat well. Wipe off spills and place them on a trivet as well.

Choosing Bowls

Most people have sets of everyday china bowls and that's what they use for any food requiring a bowl, but some bowls actually are designated for specific soups. Some soups, such as broths and creamy purees, cool down more quickly than chunky soups, and the shape of the bowls helps keep the particular soup hot or chilled. The following list describes the bowl-related items you're likely to run across. And check out Figure 16-1.

- Crocks are ovenproof bowls, sometimes with one or two handles, that are used specifically for French Onion Soup. They're also good for thick chowders and hearty legume soups.

- Double handled, deep bowls with sloped sides are known as cream soup bowls and are also used for broths and consommé. You'll find these in some formal place settings.

- Soup plates are shallow bowls, often with a wide rim. They are perfect for chowders, vegetable soups, and hearty or brothy soups with many ingredients. Some china sets include them, so you'll find that they're often used for a wide variety of soups. Note that soup cools more quickly in this type of bowl.

- Medium-size, deep bowls with sloped sides are excellent for keeping soup hot. Because they're also included in sets, they too are used for serving all kinds of soup. They're ideal for Asian noodle soups.

- Chinese soup bowls are usually porcelain and look like large rice bowls. They're deep with sharply sloped sides and a flat bottom, and they usually rest on a small pedestal. These are perfect for Hot and Sour Soup and other Asian Soups.

- Japanese soup bowls have a shape similar to Chinese soup bowls, but they're slightly fuller with a more rounded bottom. Sometimes made of lacquerware, they most often have lids. They're fine for broths and miso soups.

- Tureens are large porcelain or ceramic serving bowls with lids that are used specifically for serving soup at a buffet, on the sideboard, or at the table. Sometimes, the lid has a cut-out where a ladle can be inserted.

Figure 16-1:
Bowls,
crocks, and
tureens,
oh my!

Soup bowls should be placed on an underplate. The only exceptions are Chinese and Japanese soup bowls. Underplates are a convenient place to rest your spoon when you're finished, and they also keep the table clean if some of the soup spills. If you're worried about the bowl sliding on the plate, put a doily or a lightly dampened cocktail napkin under the bowl.

Your Final Touch: Garnishes

Garnishes are the finishing flair that you add before sending your master-piece to the table. The simpler the garnish, the better — and a little bit is all that's required. Don't spend too much time preparing them. Think of gar-nishes as punctuation, your exclamation point. They can be an accent of color, a contrasting texture, the spotlight on a flavor already in the dish, or a distinct but complementary taste.

General garnishes include chopped parsley and chives, but these suggestions for garnishes can be made in minutes:

- ✔ Finely chopped herbs or small sprigs such as basil, celery leaves, chervil, chives, cilantro, snipped dill, mint, or parsley
- ✔ Freshly ground spices such as coriander, nutmeg, black pepper, or white pepper
- ✔ Finely ground spices such as cayenne, cinnamon, garam masala, or paprika
- ✔ Fresh spices, aromatics, and chilies cut into thin strips or minced and used sparingly, such as ginger or seeded jalapeños, serranos, or cayenne chili peppers
- ✔ Tabasco or other liquid hot chili sauce

- Crushed red chili flakes
- Vegetables, finely diced or cut into thin strips, such as bell peppers, cucumber, scallions, or seeded tomatoes
- Homemade bacon bits
- Pesto
- Finely chopped sun-dried tomatoes mixed with a clove of minced garlic, a tablespoon of parsley and basil, and a little cream or olive oil to bind
- Freshly grated cheese, such as Parmesan or Romano, or crumbled blue, goat, or feta cheese
- Chopped hard-boiled eggs
- Yogurt or sour cream
- Cream or whipped cream
- Nuts, such as chopped peanuts or slivered almonds
- Croutons
- Croutes (a thick slice of toasted or fried bread)
- Citrus wedges
- Finely grated citrus zest or citrus peel cut into very thin strips, such as oranges, lemons, or limes

Appropriate garnishes are suggested in the recipes, but feel free to improvise. Choose a garnish that reflects, accentuates, balances, or complements the flavors and colors in the dish. Remember the ethnic origin of the soup, and don't put a dollop of sour cream into miso soup or sprinkle cilantro and chili flakes on borscht.

Souper Meals

Today's dining style is relaxed. Whether you're planning a meal for yourself, your family, or your company, creating a menu is easy. Put one together that will give you pleasure. Why not shoot for the stars? Ideally, you should have as much enjoyment making it as you have eating it.

Soup as a first course

In general, if your main course is light, such as grilled chicken or fish, start with a more substantial soup. If the main course is heavier, such as steak or chops, begin with a light soup. Serve it with rolls or crackers. As a first course, plan on ½ cup to 1 cup per person. Hearty soups should not be served as a first course, but only as a main course, because they are quite substantial.

Soup as a main course

When serving soup as a main course, allow extra portions for second helpings. Naturally, your serving size will go up to 1 to 2 cups. Crisp and colorful greens, grilled or chopped vegetables, and fresh fruit salad, as well as crusty bread, rolls, and focaccia, are perfect partners to most soup. You can stretch soup, whether light or hearty, to feed more people by offering sandwiches, pasta salad, quiche, or an antipasti platter of cheese, fruit, marinated or grilled vegetables, cold meats, or smoked fish, as well as an assortment of bread and crackers.

When planning a meal, keep it practical and simple. Combine items of similar ethnic origins whose flavors work in harmony.

Chapter 17

Fast Finishes

*G*arnishes are your closing statement — the finale of the dish. Although you'll often use chopped fresh herbs or nothing at all, this chapter gives you easy recipes to make your presentation a bit more appetizing.

Bacon Bits

Freshly cooked bacon bits are a wonderful addition to many soups and salads.

Level: Easy

Preparation time: 10 to 15 minutes

Do not freeze

6 slices of bacon, preferably "thick-cut," or 6 slices slab bacon, rind removed

1 Cut the bacon slices crosswise into thin strips, about ¼ to ½ inch thick.

2 Cook in a medium skillet over medium-low heat, stirring occasionally, until the bacon pieces begin to brown on all sides. With a slotted spoon, transfer the bacon to a paper towel-lined plate and blot off the excess fat.

3 When the bacon has cooled and dried, chop it into bits as shown in Figure 17-1.

Tip: *Make the bacon bits a day or two ahead of time and store in an airtight container in the refrigerator. Bring them to room temperature before using.*

Per Serving: *Calories 50.0; Protein 2.0g; Carbohydrates 0g; Dietary fiber 0g; Total fat 4.0g; Saturated fat 2.0g; Cholesterol 10.0mg; Sodium 250.0mg.*

Figure 17-1:
Makin'
bacon bits.

Pesto

Pesto isn't just for pasta; it's also a lovely complement to many tomato-based and vegetables soups.

Level: Easy

Tools: Food processor or blender

Preparation time: 10 to 15 minutes

Freezes well

2 cups fresh basil leaves	⅓ cup freshly grated Parmesan cheese
¼ cup pinenuts or chopped walnuts	⅛ teaspoon freshly ground black pepper
2 to 3 cloves garlic, peeled	½ cup extra virgin olive oil

1 In a food processor or blender, combine the basil, pinenuts, and garlic. Pulse until the ingredients form a paste. Add the Parmesan cheese and pepper and pulse until blended.

2 While the machine is running, pour the olive oil through the feeding tube or if using a blender, remove the plastic handle from the top of the blender, replace the top on the machine,and pour the olive oil through the hole. If the pesto is a bit too thick, gradually add a bit more olive oil.

Tip: Put extra pesto in an airtight plastic container and cover the top of the pesto with a thin layer of olive oil. Store in the refrigerator for 2 to 4 weeks, or freeze for up to 3 months. Allow the pesto to come to room temperature before using in any recipe. You can use leftover pesto on pasta or as a garnish for sliced mozzarella and tomato salad or on roasted bell pepper salad.

Variation: Try making pesto with other herbs such as flat-leaf, Italian parsley or cilantro. If using parsley, add the finely grated zest of ½ medium lemon. Use this pesto in place of basil pesto. If using cilantro, omit the Parmesan and use ⅓ cup walnuts and ⅓ to ½ cup olive oil. Add 1 to 2 seeded and minced jalapeño or serrano chilies and use for Mexican, Latin American, or even southeast Asian dishes.

Per Serving: Calories 83.1; Protein 1.5g; Carbohydrates 0.7g; Dietary fiber 0.3g; Total fat 8.5g; Saturated fat 1.5g; Cholesterol 1.6mg; Sodium 38.8mg.

Baked Croutes or Croutons

Croutes and croutons are traditionally used in many soups, hors d'oeuvres, and salads. The difference between the two is shown in Figure 17-2.

Level: *Easy*

Preparation time: *15 minutes*

Do not freeze

For Croutes:

French or Italian bread or sourdough bread (or any tightly grained white bread)

1 Preheat the oven to 375° F.

2 Cut the bread into slices about ½- to ¾-inch thick.

3 Arrange in a single layer on a baking sheet and brush lightly with olive oil.

4 Bake, turning once, until lightly golden and crisp, about 8 to 12 minutes.

Per Serving: Calories 100.4; Protein 2.6g; Carbohydrates 14.9g; Dietary fiber 0.8g; Total fat 3.3g; Saturated fat 0.6g; Cholesterol 0mg; Sodium 173.3mg.

For Croutons:

French, sourdough, Italian, or simple white or whole wheat loaf bread

1 Preheat the oven to 375° F.

2 Cut bread into cubes.

3 Put a small amount of olive oil in a bowl. Toss the bread in the olive oil.

4 Arrange in a single layer on a baking sheet and bake, turning once, until lightly golden and crisp, about 8 to 12 minutes.

For Herbed Croutes or Croutons: Add a small amount of dried herbs, such as basil, thyme, or crushed rosemary, to the olive oil that you use to brush onto the croutes or toss the croutons in.

Variation: To make oil-free croutes or croutons: Preheat the oven to 200 degrees F. Put the croutes or croutons on a baking sheet and bake, turning once, until dried out.

Per Serving: Calories 50.4; Protein 0.9g; Carbohydrates 5.5g; Dietary fiber 0.4g; Total fat 2.7g; Saturated fat 0.4g; Cholesterol 0mg; Sodium 52.4mg.

CROÛTES

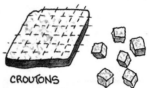

CROUTONS

Figure 17-2:
Croutons
and croutes.

Oven Toasted Bread

This is an easy way to toast bread that is too thick or the wrong shape for your toaster. You can also make more than two or four slices at a time.

Level: *Easy*

Preparation time: *5 to 10 minutes*

Do not freeze

1 Preheat the oven to 375° F to 400° F.

2 Place bread slices on a baking sheet and bake until lightly toasted, turning once.

Tip: *Crush extra toast into breadcrumbs and store in an airtight container in the refrigerator for up to 2 weeks.*

Per Serving: *Calories 80.5; Protein 2.6g; Carbohydrates 14.9g; Dietary fiber 0.8g; Total fat 1.1g; Saturated fat 0.3g; Cholesterol 0mg; Sodium 173.3mg.*

Parsley Dumplings

Turn a simple broth into a meal by adding flavorful dumplings. Garnish your soup with a little freshly grated Romano or Parmesan cheese and freshly chopped parsley!

Level: *Easy to intermediate*

Preparation time: *10 to 15 minutes*

Makes about 6 dumplings

Do not freeze

1 cup all-purpose flour

1½ teaspoons baking powder

½ teaspoon salt

2 tablespoons finely chopped fresh flat-leaf or Italian parsley

½ teaspoon finely chopped fresh thyme or rosemary

⅛ teaspoon freshly ground white or black pepper

2 ½ tablespoons chilled butter or margarine

⅓ cup milk (plus 1 to 2 tablespoons more if needed)

1 Sift the flour, baking powder, and salt. Add the parsley, thyme, and pepper and stir to mix evenly.

2 Cut the butter into the flour mixture using two forks or a dough blender until it resembles coarse cornmeal. Add enough of the milk to make a thick batter that you can mound on a small soup spoon. (you might need a tablespoon or two more milk than indicated, and if you do, you'll need to add it a tablepoon at a time.)

3 To cook the dumplings, mound the batter onto a small spoon and drop them into 6 cups of simmering broth. Cook in the gently bubbling broth for 5 to 10 minutes or until the dumplings are set and cooked through.

Per Serving: Calories 80.5; Protein 2.6g; Carbohydrates 14.9g; Dietary fiber 0.8g; Total fat 1.1g; Saturated fat 0.3g; Cholesterol 0mg; Sodium 173.3mg.

Part VI

The Part of Tens

The 5th Wave   By Rich Tennant

COOKBOOKS TO AVOID

CLASSIC New England Boiled Desserts

PASTA ON THE GRILL WITH Rolf

HEADCHEESE HEADCHEESE and more HEADCHEESE at the Gilmore Inn

Technique de Manifold

Cooking on your engine block the French way!

In this part . . .

1 provide you with ten ways to fix soup mistakes, and I offer you ten ideas for pairing various soups with other courses in your meals.

Chapter 18

Ten Ways to Fix Soup Faux Pas

● ●

In This Chapter

▶ Giving first aid to salty and overseasoned soup

▶ Finding the right balance of flavor and texture

● ●

*W*ell, you were supposed to simmer slowly, but you had the heat so high that the liquid evaporated while you were relaxing in the tub or in front of the tube. Or you've added too much salt. Oops! Or maybe you forgot to put the cover on, or you covered it and it boiled over, spilling out some of the precious broth onto the stovetop. Okay, you just really had trouble making your soup "just so." The hints in this chapter help you make it "just right." This chapter is full of remedies for common mistakes.

Doubling the fun

Suppose that you stubbed your toe when you approached the pot with the salt, and now the soup's too salty. What do you do? If you have time, make a second batch without salt and combine the two. Taste and adjust the salt, but be careful this time! You'll definitely have soup for your freezer. This method also works if you've added too much of any strong seasoning herbs and spices such as curry, cayenne, pepper, oregano, or rosemary.

Getting a second chance

If the soup you've made is only a little bit salty, add more broth or water and simmer a while longer.

Adding a potato

To over-salted soup, add a peeled, raw potato that has been quartered, and simmer for 15 minutes. Remove the potato with a slotted spoon, and discard before serving. The potato will absorb some of the salt.

Tricking your taste buds

Yes, you can fool your taste buds! All you have to do is to add a little sweetness — either white granulated sugar or brown sugar. Start by adding ¼ teaspoon, and taste the soup until the seasonings are adjusted to your liking.

Getting thinner

Most of us like thick soups, but not soups that you need a knife to eat! Fix a soup that's too thick with this tip: Add more broth, water, milk, or whatever liquid was used for the soup. Simmer until the soup is heated through and the flavor is balanced.

Plumping up

A soup that's too thin just screams for more body. These suggestions help you know what to do.

Increase the heat slightly and simmer, uncovered, until it's the right consistency. But don't boil the soup rapidly.

You can puree some of the soup in a blender or food processor and return it to the pot, or add mild-tasting, pureed vegetables, such as mashed potatoes, or ingredients such as pureed cooked rice. (Puree the rice in the blender with some of the soup.) If the recipe is for a pureed soup, add additional cooked, pureed vegetables that you've already used in the recipe.

Bringing bread to the rescue

Another easy way to thicken a soup is to add a few fresh breadcrumbs. You can make them in seconds by crumbling fresh bread (without the crust) between your fingers or by pulsing the bread in a food processor.

Adding texture

Change the texture of thin or thick soup by making it creamy. Add cream or a dollop of sour cream or yogurt.

Handling boilovers

If the soup's boiled over, first turn off the burner and clean up the mess so that it doesn't bake into the surface of the stove. Then return the soup to the heat, and add enough broth to make the desired consistency. Reduce the heat to medium-low and simmer, partially covered, until the flavors are blended. Taste for seasoning, and adjust if necessary.

Fixing an undercooked soup

If the veggies are a bit hard or the meat's tough, the soup is underdone — even if you've cooked it as long as a recipe suggests. More than likely, the burner's heat has been too low for too long. This sometimes happens with electric stoves when currents fluctuate. Increase the heat slightly, and continue simmering until the ingredients are tender and the soup acquires the right consistency.

Chapter 19

Ten Souperb Pairings

In This Chapter

▶ Serving and menu suggestions for several soup recipes

▶ Matching beverages with soup

Maybe friends are coming to eat, or maybe you just want to plan a simple family gathering featuring soup as the main course. In this chapter, you'll find ten suggestions to help you make soup the star of your meal.

South of the Border Black Bean Soup and . . .

You'll find this recipe in Chapter 8. Kick off the menu with salsa, tortilla chips, and guacamole. Serve both the starters and the soup with plenty of *cerveza*, known north of the border as beer.

Spicy Pumpkin and Corn Chowder and . . .

You'll find this recipe in Chapter 9. This soup makes use of autumn's harvest. Serve it with warm biscuits and a salad of romaine lettuce tossed in a creamy dressing. A cup of mulled or plain warm cider and homemade cookies are a tasty finale.

Creamy Cheddar Cheese Soup and . . .

You'll find this recipe in Chapter 10. A loaf of crusty French bread or a few slices of rye bread and a tossed green salad with a vinaigrette or Italian dressing is all that's needed for a simple lunch or supper. All you need to do is add a beverage. Although cheese and wine is a classic combination, and any full-bodied red wine such as a Cabernet or Burgundy will do the soup justice, I prefer to serve this soup with ale or beer. End the meal with fresh fruit.

Nana's Beef, Vegetable, and Barley Soup and . . .

You'll find this soup in Chapter 11. This filling, stand-alone soup requires no side dishes, but you may serve it with fresh rolls and your favorite beverage. End the meal with a warm fruit cobbler or fruit crisp garnished with a dollop of whipped cream.

Herbed Oxtail and Vegetable Soup and . . .

You'll find this recipe in Chapter 11. With the addition of a roasted vegetable salad and fresh bread for dunking in the flavorful broth, you'll have a great meal. Serve it with a good red wine such as merlot. End the meal with a refreshing sorbet.

Chicken and Sausage Gumbo and . . .

You'll find this recipe in Chapter 11. Pair it with a bean salad garnished with sliced ripe tomatoes, and serve it with iced tea or beer. For dessert, how about lemon chess pie or pecan pie?

Sicilian Fish Soup and . . .

You'll find this recipe in Chapter 14. Serve the soup with plenty of extra country-style bread and an Italian white wine such as Frascati or Bolla Soave. Finish the meal with fresh fruit and cheese.

Italian Chicken, Greens, and Tortellini Soup and . . .

You'll find this recipe in Chapter 14. Serve it with sparkling spring water garnished with a wedge of lemon. Finish the meal with a slice of hazelnut cake or a few biscotti and a cup of cappuccino.

French Onion Soup and . . .

You'll find this recipe in Chapter 14. I like to serve white wine such as a chardonnay or chablis, but if you feel extravagant, by all means serve sparkling wine or champagne. Some versions of this soup call for champagne in the soup instead of the white wine I suggest. Add a salad of mixed baby greens tossed with oil and vinegar and your menu's set, but feel free to indulge in chocolate mousse or crème brûlée for dessert.

Hearty Winter Borscht and . . .

You'll find this recipe in Chapter 14. Start off the evening with a chilled cocktail — made with vodka, of course. Serve the soup with potato bread or rolls. End the meal with baked apples garnished with custard or whipped cream.

Metric Conversion Guide

*N*ote: The recipes in this cookbook were not developed or tested using metric measures. There may be some variation in quality when converting to metric units.

Common Abbreviations

Abbreviation(s)	What It Stands For
C, c	cup
g	gram
kg	kilogram
L, l	liter
lb	pound
mL, ml	milliliter
oz	ounce
pt	pint
t, tsp	teaspoon
T, TB, Tbl, Tbsp	tablespoon

Volume

U.S. Units	Canadian Metric	Australian Metric
¼ teaspoon	1 mL	1 ml
½ teaspoon	2 mL	2 ml
1 teaspoon	5 mL	5 ml
1 tablespoon	15 mL	20 ml
¼ cup	50 mL	60 ml
⅓ cup	75 mL	80 ml
½ cup	125 mL	125 ml
⅔ cup	150 mL	170 ml
¾ cup	175 mL	190 ml
1 cup	250 mL	250 ml
1 quart	1 liter	1 liter
1½ quarts	1.5 liters	1.5 liters
2 quarts	2 liters	2 liters
2½ quarts	2.5 liters	2.5 liters
3 quarts	3 liters	3 liters
4 quarts	4 liters	4 liters

Weight

U.S. Units	Canadian Metric	Australian Metric
1 ounce	30 grams	30 grams
2 ounces	55 grams	60 grams
3 ounces	85 grams	90 grams
4 ounces (¼ pound)	115 grams	125 grams
8 ounces (½ pound)	225 grams	225 grams
16 ounces (1 pound)	455 grams	500 grams
1 pound	455 grams	½ kilogram

Measurements

Inches	Centimeters
½	1.5
1	2.5
2	5.0
3	7.5
4	10.0
5	12.5
6	15.0
7	17.5
8	20.5
9	23.0
10	25.5
11	28.0
12	30.5
13	33.0

Temperature (Degrees)	
Fahrenheit	Celsius
32	0
212	100
250	120
275	140
300	150
325	160
350	180
375	190
400	200
425	220
450	230
475	240
500	260

Index

• *C* •

• D •

• H •

• I •

• Y •

• Z •

WWW.DUMMIES.COM

Discover Dummies Online!

The Dummies Web Site is your fun and friendly online resource for the latest information about *For Dummies*® books and your favorite topics. The Web site is the place to communicate with us, exchange ideas with other *For Dummies* readers, chat with authors, and have fun!

Ten Fun and Useful Things You Can Do at www.dummies.com

1. Win free *For Dummies* books and more!
2. Register your book and be entered in a prize drawing.
3. Meet your favorite authors through the IDG Books Worldwide Author Chat Series.
4. Exchange helpful information with other *For Dummies* readers.
5. Discover other great *For Dummies* books you must have!
6. Purchase Dummieswear® exclusively from our Web site.
7. Buy *For Dummies* books online.
8. Talk to us. Make comments, ask questions, get answers!
9. Download free software.
10. Find additional useful resources from authors.

Link directly to these ten fun and useful things at
http://www.dummies.com/10useful

For other technology titles from IDG Books Worldwide, go to
www.idgbooks.com

Not on the Web yet? It's easy to get started with *Dummies 101*®: *The Internet For Windows*® *98* or *The Internet For Dummies*® at local retailers everywhere.

Find other *For Dummies* books on these topics:

Business • Career • Databases • Food & Beverage • Games • Gardening • Graphics • Hardware
Health & Fitness • Internet and the World Wide Web • Networking • Office Suites
Operating Systems • Personal Finance • Pets • Programming • Recreation • Sports
Spreadsheets • Teacher Resources • Test Prep • Word Processing

IDG BOOKS WORLDWIDE
BOOK REGISTRATION

Register This Book and Win!

We want to hear from you!

Visit **http://my2cents.dummies.com** to register this book and tell us how you liked it!

- Get entered in our monthly prize giveaway.

- Give us feedback about this book — tell us what you like best, what you like least, or maybe what you'd like to ask the author and us to change!

- Let us know any other *For Dummies*® topics that interest you.

Your feedback helps us determine what books to publish, tells us what coverage to add as we revise our books, and lets us know whether we're meeting your needs as a *For Dummies* reader. You're our most valuable resource, and what you have to say is important to us!

Not on the Web yet? It's easy to get started with *Dummies 101*®: *The Internet For Windows*® *98* or *The Internet For Dummies*® at local retailers everywhere.

Or let us know what you think by sending us a letter at the following address:

For Dummies Book Registration
Dummies Press
10475 Crosspoint Blvd.
Indianapolis, IN 46256

BESTSELLING BOOK SERIES